Silent Temples, Songful Hearts:
Traditional Music of Cambodia

Silent Temples, Songful Hearts:
Traditional Music of Cambodia

Sam-Ang Sam
Patricia Shehan Campbell

World Music Press

Silent Temples, Songful Hearts:
Traditional Music of Cambodia
by
Sam-Ang Sam
Patricia Shehan Campbell

World Music Press
Multicultural Materials for Educators
Judith Cook Tucker, Publisher; Editor-in-Chief
PO Box 2565 Danbury CT 06813-2565
(203) 748-1131

Original Paperback Edition
Printed in the United States of America on acid-free paper by
the Princeton University Press, Princeton NJ
1 2 3 4 5

Music engraved by Don Wallace using Music Prose® version 2.1
Typeset by Judith Cook Tucker using a Macintosh IIci and Pagemaker® v. 4.01

Library of Congress Cataloging-in-Publication Data

Sam, Sam-Ang, 1950-
    Silent temples, songful hearts : traditional music of Cambodia/
  Sam-Ang Sam and Patricia Shehan Campbell; [illustrations by Yang Sam
and Tho "Tony" Sangphet ; photographs by Bonnie Periale, Winnie
Lambrecht, Sam-Ang Sam]. -- Original pbk ed.
          p.   cm.
Discography: p.
Filmography: p.
Includes bibliographical references (p.) and index.
ISBN 0-937203-36-x (pbk./tape : acid-free paper) :
ISBN 0-937203-37-8 (pbk. : acid-free paper) :
ISBN 0-937203-38-6 (audio cassette) :
1. Folk music--Cambodia--History and criticism. I. Campbell,
Patricia Shehan. II. Title.
ML3758.C16S2   1991
781.62'9593--dc20   91-34994
                                                                    MN

About the Authors

Sam-Ang Sam, Ph.D. is one of the very few remaining Khmer master artists who are alive and able to practice and teach their traditions. He was born in Krakor, in Pursat province. He showed a strong interest in music from early childhood, and was enrolled in formal studies of traditional Khmer music at age 14 when he entered the University of Fine Arts in Phnom Penh, Cambodia, in the early 1960's, obtaining instrumental instruction from Masters Yim Sem, Yim Saing, Sek Ouch, and Long Samreth. He also had vocal training provided by Mistress Ham Nam and Master Ros Lorn. During his two-year residency in Siem Reap province, Sam-Ang Sam learned the *sralai* (quadruple-reed shawm), now his principal instrument, from Master Thoeung and Master Chhuon.

Sam-Ang Sam graduated with the degree of Diplôme des Arts and Baccalauréat des Arts in 1970 and 1973 respectively from the University of Fine Arts in Phnom Penh. In 1974 he was awarded a fellowship by the Cambodian Government to further his study in Western Music Composition at the University of the Philippines, under the guidance of Eliseo Pajaro and Ramon Santos. While at the University of the Philippines, he also had his first exposure to ethnomusicology while attending classes on Philippine music offered by Jose Maceda. From there he came to the United States in 1977 and continued his study at Connecticut College where he received both the BA and MA degrees in Music Composition under the tutelage of Chinary Ung, Noel Zahler and Arthur Welwood. Sam-Ang Sam then enrolled at Wesleyan University and received his Ph.D. degree in Ethnomusicology.

He is a scholar on Khmer music, and with his wife, dancer Chan Moly Sam, has jointly written two books on Khmer music and dance published by the Khmer Studies Institute. He has performed on a number of sound recordings on the labels of the Khmer Studies Institute, Cambodian Business Corporation International, World Music Institute, and the Center for the Study of Khmer Culture. He has performed in Asia, Europe, and the United States, including the White House in 1985.

In recognition of his dedication to the preservation and maintenance of Khmer culture and scholarship, Sam-Ang Sam has received several awards and grants, including the Arts and Culture preservation Award, Social Science Research Council grants, National Endowment for the Arts grants, the Ford Foundation/Asian Cultural Council grants, and the Middletown Commission on the Arts Grant. He frequently travels to Cambodian communities throughout North America to perform traditional music for dances, festivals, and various ceremonies requiring particular music. He is currently Artist-in-Residence at the University of Washington.

Patricia Shehan Campbell, Ph.D. is Associate Professor of Music and Chair of Music Education at the University of Washington. She received her Ph.D. in music education with a concentration in ethnomusicology from Kent State University, where she studied South Indian mridangam and Karnatic vocal techniques with Ramnad V. Raghavan, played in the Thai Ensemble and studied Laotian kaen with Terry Miller and Jarernchai Chonpairot. Her interest in world music has taken her as a student, researcher and clinician to Bulgaria, Hungary, India, Japan, China and Australia.

Dr. Campbell is a consultant on music in early and middle childhood, multicultural music education, and the use of movement as a pedagogical tool. She is author of numerous publications that blend ethnomusicological and educational issues, including *Lessons from the World* (1991), *Sounds of the World: Music of Eastern Europe* (1989) and *Sounds of the World: Music of Southeast Asia* (1986). She co-authored *From Rice Paddies and Temple Yards: Traditional Music of Vietnam* (with Phong Nguyen, 1990) and *Multicultural Perspectives in Music Education* (with William M. Anderson, 1989). She served as a consultant for the NEA-funded project that studied Laotian resettlement in the U.S. resulting in the film *Silk Sarongs and City Streets*. She is an active member of the College Music Society, the International Society for Music Education, The Dalcroze Society of America, the Organization of Kodaly Educators, the American Orff-Schulwerk Association and the Society for Ethnomusicology (chair of the Education Committee and a member of the SEM Council). She also serves on the editorial board of the *Journal of Research in Music Education* of the Music Educators National Conference.

Forward

From the perspective of a society inclined to cut funding to the arts at the drop of a budget, it is difficult to understand why the Khmer value their arts so highly. For the typical American community, the arts are the first area cut during a fiscal crisis; in Cambodia they were the first aspects of culture to be restored after liberation from the Khmer Rouge in 1979. Music, song, and dance for the Khmer are not merely pleasant diversions which have a place only after all other needs have been filled; they have a near-sacred status and constitute a major component of Khmer identity.

During a week-long visit to Cambodia in late 1988, I had the privilege of observing dancers and musicians from the University of Fine Arts perform in a former dance pavilion at the palace in Phnom Penh. Most performers were young; a few older masters had survived the holocaust. This performance was not something that could be taken for granted. It represented a part of the rebirth of the Khmer culture from the ashes of death and destruction wrought by the radical Khmer Rouge, who had sought to obliterate Khmer culture; they nearly succeeded. In many ways this restoration precedes the physical rebuilding of the country. Evidently that sacred link with the collective spirit of the Khmer people is so strongly expressed through music and dance that these arts must be rebuilt before material things are given any attention.

Dr. Sam-Ang Sam, co-author of this book, together with his wife and daughters, have been the leading figures in the United States seeking to keep Khmer music and dance alive. They have taught and performed widely and written about their arts. They have encouraged older musicians who came as refugees to keep performing and with them have given many performances. These efforts to make Khmer music known to the younger generation are of the utmost importance. Being Cambodian-American means keeping the best of the old culture and adopting the best of the new. Considering the importance of the arts to Khmer identity, this book has the added significance of helping young Cambodian-Americans understand who they are and where they came from.

Terry E. Miller
Center for the Study of World Musics
Kent State University

Table of Contents

About the Authors, 5
Forward, 7
List of Musical Transcriptions, 9
List of Illustrations, 9
List of Photographs, 10
Contents of the Companion Tape, 11
Preface, 13
Notes, 15
Romanization of Khmer Words, 17
Maps, 20

Chapter 1.   Historical and Cultural Background, 19-26
          Geography—Climate—Economy—History—
          Exodus from Cambodia—Communities in United States

Chapter 2.   Customs and Traditions, 27-36
          Religion—Ethnic Makeup—Language—Family—Clothing—
          Festivals—Education—The Arts

Chapter 3.   Khmer Musical Forms, Genres and Instruments, 37-56
          Music in Historical Perspective—Musical Characteristics—Musical
          Instruments: Aerophones, Idiophones, Membranophones, Chordophones—
          Musical Forms and Genres—Tradition and Change—Teaching and Learning

Chapter 4.   A Guide to the Music of Cambodia: Fourteen Guided
          Listening Experiences, 57-
          Introduction—For the Music Professional—Performance Considerations
          When Using Classroom Instruments—Learning by Listening

          I.   Three Etiquette Songs for Small Children: "Mun Pel Nhaim" [Before Mealtime]
                    "Doeur Roeu Keng" [Walk or Sleep]; "Leang Dai" [Wash Hands], 63
          II.   A Game Song: "Chapp Kaun Khleng" [Catch the Baby Eagle], 67
          III.   Scarf Game Songs: "Leak Kanseng" [Hiding the Scarf] and "Chhoung," 71
          IV.   Song of the Colorful Bird: "Sarika Keo," 76
          V.   Khmer Action Song: "Bakkha" [Bird], 80
          VI.   Beginners Instrumental Piece: "Thung Le," 84
          VII.   A Sampler of Instrumental Sounds, 87
          VIII. Piece for Three Instruments: *Roneat Ek, Korng Tauch, Korng Thomm,* 91
          IX.   The *Mohori* Ensemble: "Khvann Tung," 96
          X.   A Musical Story: "The Story of Neang Kangrey and Prince Rithisen," 101
          XI.   Drums: Themes and Variations on the *Thaun-Rumanea* Drum Pair, 105
          XII.   Boxing Music: "Phleng Pradall," 108
          XIII. Popular Music/Popular Dance: *Roam Vung,* 111
          XIV.   The Legend of Tiger, 114

Appendix: Transcriptions in the Key of Recorded Performance, 117
Glossary, 121
Selected Bibliography-Discography-Filmography, 138-141
Index, 143

List of Musical Transcriptions

1. "Mun Pel Nhaim" [Before Mealtime], 63
2. "Doeur Roeu Keng" [Walk or Sleep], 64
3. "Leang Dai" [Wash Hands], 64
4. "Chapp Kaun Khleng" [Catch the Baby Eagle], 68
5. "Leak Kanseng" [Hiding the Scarf], 71
6. "Chhoung," 72
7. "Sarika Keo," 77
8. "Bakkha" [Bird], 82
9. "Thung Le," 86
10. "Khmer Changkeh Reav," 92
11. "Khvann Tung," 98
12. "Khvann Tung" scales relating to the piece, 100
13. "Khvann Tung" principal pitches of the piece, 100
14. "Loeung Preah Punlea," 103
15. Themes and Variations of the *Thaun-Rumanea* Drum Pair, 106-107

List of Illustrations

Map of Southeast Asia, 20
Map of Cambodia, 20
Angkor Vatt (Yang Sam), 28
Jayavarman VII (Yang Sam), 28
Bayan Temple (Yang Sam), 28
Buddhist Monk (Yang Sam), 32
Apsara (celestial figure from Angkor Vatt) (Yang Sam), 35
Leather Shadow puppets, 36
Pey praboh (Yang Sam), 40
Sralai (Yang Sam), 42
Tror ou (Yang Sam), 46
Robaim nesat. [trap-fishing dance](Yang Sam), 49
Robaim chraut srauv [harvest dance] (Yang Sam), 50
Staging the Shadow Play (Yang Sam), 56
Traditional canoe in water lillies (Tho Sangphet), 62
Boy and Girl in traditional clothing (Yang Sam), 66
Children playing "Chapp Kaun Khleng" (Yang Sam), 68
Children playing "Leak Kanseng" (Yang Sam), 70
Young adults playing "Chhoung" (Yang Sam), 70
Tiger (Yang Sam), 74
Sarika keo (Tho Sangphet), 76
Hand gesture (Yang Sam), 81
Cattle herder playing *khloy* as water buffalo walks by (Tho Sangphet), 84
The Giantess Santhamea (Tho Sangphet), 101
Mask of Giant (Yang Sam), 102
Sralai (Sam-Ang Sam), 108
Robaim tralok [coconut shell dance] (Yang Sam), 110
Tiger (Yang Sam), 115

List of Photographs

Sam-Ang Sam, 5
Patricia Shehan Campbell, 5
The countryside of Cambodia, 22
Morning street activities, Phnom Penh, 22
Young people rehearsing a folk dance at Jacob's Pillow, 32
Chan Moly Sam and Somaly Hay perform an *Apsara* dance, 35
Phon Bin demonstrating *roneat ek*, 43
Sam-Ang Sam playing *khloy*, 43
Phon Bin demonstrating *krapeu*, 43
Phon Bin demonstrating *khimm*, 43
Thaun-rumanea drum pair, 44
Sampho, 44
Skor arakk, 44
Chhing, 44
Roneat thung, 44
Korng thomm, 44
Pinn peat ensemble (part), 44
Phon Bin demonstrating *tror Khmer*, 47
A *tror so tauch* player, 47
Phon Bin demonstrating the *chapey dang veng* lute, 47
Muni Mekhala Dance Drama (L. and R.), 48
Chan Moly Sam wearing *mkott*, 49
Court dance hand gesture meaning flower, 49
Traditional wedding, Danbury CT, 51
Musicians at traditional wedding, Danbury CT, 51
Laim leav dance - popular dance, 54
Sek Sarika [parrot dance] gestures demonstrated by Laksmi Sam, 80
Chan Moly Sam and young students, 81
Malene Sam warming up for court dancing, 81
Pinn peat ensemble showing *korng tauch* and *korng thomm*, 91
Sam-Ang Sam playing *roneat ek*, 95
Mohori ensemble, 97
Roneat ek, 97
Thaun-rumanea drum pair, 105
Chann Chhaya Dance Pavilion, 111
Malene Sam demonstrating *roam vung* dance steps, 112

Contents of the Companion Tape

Tape Cut	Lesson	Title	Performer(s)
Side A:			
1.	1	"Mun Pel Nhaim"	Malene Sam, Laksmi Sam, vocals
			Sam-Ang Sam, *tror so*
			Music : Sam-Ang Sam
			Lyrics: Yang Sam
2.	1	"Doeur Roeu Keng"	Malene Sam, Laksmi Sam, vocals
			Sam-Ang Sam, *tror so*
3.	1	"Leang Dai"	Malene Sam, Laksmi Sam, vocals
			Sam-Ang Sam, *tror so*
4.	2	"Chapp Kaun Khleng"	Malene, Laksmi, Sam-Ang Sam, voc..
5.	3	"Leak Kanseng"	Malene, Laksmi, Sam-Ang Sam, voc.
6.	3	"Chhoung"	Sam-Ang Sam, vocal
7.	4	"Sarika Keo"	Malene Sam, Laksmi Sam vocals
			Sam-Ang Sam, *tror so*
8.	5	"Bakkha (Baksa)"	Malene Sam, Laksmi Sam, vocals
			Sam-Ang Sam, *roneat ek*
9-A.	6	"Thung Le"	Sam-Ang Sam, *khloy*
9-B.	6	"Thung Le"	Sam-Ang Sam, *roneat ek*
10-A.	7	*khloy*: "Khmer Changkeh Reav"	Sam-Ang Sam, *khloy*
10-B.	7	*pey pork*: "Surin"	Sam-Ang Sam, *pey pork*
10-C.	7	*sralai:* "Chhouy Chhay"	Sam-Ang Sam, *sralai*
10-D.	7	*tror so*: "Khyall Chumno Khe Praing"	Sam-Ang Sam, *tror so*
10-E.	7	*khimm*: "Locung Preah Punlea"	Sam-Ang Sam, *khimm*
10-F.	7	*roneat ek:* "Khmer Krang Phka"	Sam-Ang Sam, *roneat ek*
10-G.	7	*roneat thung*: "Chenn Choh Touk"	Sam-Ang Sam, *roneat thung*
10-H.	7	*korng vung*: "Sinuon"	David Hunter, *korng tauch*
10-I.	7	*chhing*: pattern	Sam-Ang Sam, *chinng*
11-A.	8	ensemble: "Khmer Changkeh Reav"	Sam-Ang Sam, *roneat ek*
			David Hunter, *korng tauch*
			Rita Hutajulu, *korng thomm*
11-B.	8	*roneat ek*, basic melody "Khmer Changkeh Reav"	Sam-Ang Sam, *roneat ek*
11-C.	8	*roneat ek*, elaborated melody "Khmer Changkeh Reav"	Sam-Ang Sam, *roneat ek*
11-D.	8	*korng tauch:* "Khmer Changkeh Reav"	David Hunter, *korng tauch*
11-E.	8	*korng thomm* "Khmer Changkeh Reav"	Rita Hutajulu, *korng thomm*

Tape Cut Side B:	Lesson	Title	Performer(s)
11-F.	8	ensemble "Khmer Changkeh Reav"	SAS, DH, RH (as in 11-A)
12.	9	"Khvann Tung"	Sam-Ang Sam, vocal
13.	10	"Loeung Preah Punlea"	Sam-Ang Sam, vocal
14-A.	11	Drums: *Thaun-Rumanea* *Level one rhythm pattern and drum syllables [8-beat] *Level one rhythm pattern (8-beat), embellished	Sam-Ang Sam, *thaun-rumanea*
14-B.	11	Drums: *Thaun-Rumanea* *Level two rhythm pattern and drum syllables (16-beat) *Level two rhythm pattern drum syllables (16-beat), embellished	Sam-Ang Sam, *thaun-rumanea*
15.	12	"Phleng Pradall" [Boxing Music]	Sam-Ang Sam, *sralai* Malene Sam, *chhing*
16.	13	"Anhcheunh Loeung Roam"	Saroeun Chey, vocal Words/music: Sam-Ang Sam
17.	14	The Legend of Tiger	Narrated by Laksmi Sam

Preface

This book and its companion tape are intended as an introduction to traditional Khmer music and culture in Cambodia and as preserved in Cambodian-American communities in the United States, and is the first of its kind to be published in the English language. The book contributes to an understanding of the Khmer people through chapters on their history and geography, their long-standing customs, and their performing arts of music, dance and theater. So to allow the reader an ease of entrance into a world of uniquely beautiful musical and artistic expressions, we introduce a composite of traditional Khmer attitudes and practices regarding religion, language, family, festivals and education. Likewise, so as to allow the listener a comprehensive view of the songs and musical selections belonging to Khmer culture, we discuss its evolution and innovation over time and as a result of the experiences which recently-arrived Cambodian-Americans have known. The fourteen sections in the last chapter are designed for the teaching of Khmer music, and Khmer culture through music. We maintain that the essence of Cambodia can be captured in song and sound; the guided lessons enable young people and adults, Khmer and non-Khmer, to know the beauty and logic of Khmer musical traditions.

While the book provides information about Khmer traditions, the heart of the culture is found in the musical sound. The accompanying tape provides the listener with recorded examples of all the Khmer music featured in the text, from folksongs and songs of childhood to solo instrumental pieces to art music of the court ensembles to the pop-rock sound of the *roam vung*. Performers include Sam-Ang Sam, his daughters Malene Sam and Laksmi Sam, his students, as well as Cambodian-American members of the *mohori* ensemble. They sing and play in a manner that conveys a reverence and love for the crystalline simplicity of some pieces and the intricate complexities of others. The listener is invited to absorb the sound, language, and mood of these pieces by listening first—without explanation. The book can best complement the listening experience when it is read later, when it can serve to enhance and guide the earlier musical exposure. Matters of pronunciation, elisions, and gliding tones will settle in the ears when the emphasis is on aural learning rather than on deciphering notation that is incapable of accurately graphing subtleties of the total sound.

We feel that the beauty of Khmer music is not to be preserved as a museum piece, set high upon a "do-not-touch" pedestal with its practices kept out of reach and unattainable by those outside the tradition. Rather, we would hope that the Khmer and the non-Khmer alike would become enlightened of one of the world's great traditional and ancient cultures through its music. Refugees and their families in Cambodian enclaves in California, Massachusetts, Washington, Minnesota, and in east- and west-coast cities are quickly becoming assimilated into mainstream American culture yet they yearn to hold on to their heritage. Some seek resources that will enable them to transmit traditional

Khmer music and culture to Khmer children in community centers, church schools, and after-school settings. Teachers of music, the arts, history and social studies in public and private schools as well, seek material that will guide students to an understanding of the lives of some of their newest classmates. Ethnomusicologists and adult students of Southeast Asian culture and music will find information on musical structure and style, as well as cultural context. The homes, farms, fields, shops, schools, and temples which Khmer students or their families left behind in Cambodia just over a decade ago are often silent today, yet the memories of their mother country are strong and stored for safekeeping in their hearts. We believe that by being exposed to and absorbing the songs, the Khmer culture will be revealed to students of every age. We thus offer *Silent Temples, Songful Hearts: Traditional Music of Cambodia* as a tribute to the beauty and strength of the Khmer people, with the aim of enriching the lives of all those who listen to their music.

Sam-Ang Sam and Patricia Shehan Campbell
Seattle, Washington
August, 1991

Notes

Musical Transcriptions: When attempting to pour a musical tradition like that of Cambodia into the mold of Western notation several problems arise:

➤The notation of songs and instrumental pieces only *approximates* the pitches of the recordings in many cases, because the instruments used in the recording were adjusted to be in tune with each other, but do not necessarily match a piano or tuning fork. Rather than artificially altering the pitches by digitally re-mastering the tape, we have decided to leave the recording as actually performed. This poses the problem of offering a transcription that is easy to read but in a slightly different key from the recording, or including a transcription that is exactly the same as the recording but might include several sharps or flats, and moreover cannot then be played on soprano recorder or the Orff Schulwerk instrumentarium by young students. In general, we have included a performable transcription in a key closest to that on the tape, and also indicated the original key. In the few cases where being able to play along with the tape seemed an important option, we have included a transcription in the performed key in an appendix toward the end of the book. (See "Musical Transcriptions in the Key of Recorded Performance," Appendix.)

➤Another difficulty encountered in trying to "trap" the performance is that the music of Cambodia is not meant to be "frozen" in any one version through notation; it is alive, dynamic and ever-evolving. The slides, slurs, embellishments and improvisations are central to the instruments, voices and tradition, but by nature problematic and actually inappropriate to fully notate for a collection such as this. As with jazz or the music of Africa, the listener might hear these pieces played precisely this way once and then never again. Rather than etch all of the nuances and musical embroidery of these individual performances in stone, we have opted to notate a simple, bare-bones transcription, stripped to the skeleton—the essence of the piece.

Transcription of Khmer words: There is no consistency in the Romanization of Khmer words; transcription varies from one writer to the next. Despite the complexities and variety of phonemes within the Khmer language, we have devised a system that is consistent throughout the pages of this book. (See "Romanization of Khmer Words," next section.)

Phonetic Pronunciation: The Khmer language has sounds that a native English speaker will barely be able to distinguish, let alone pronounce from an approximate transcription. The sounds in some cases are actually impossible to write accurately using the English alphabet. We had many discussions about how to sing certain words or phrases, and more on how to "describe" them phonetically. (See "Romanization of Khmer Words," next section.) Staying true to traditional transmission processes in Cambodia, we agreed that the music and pronunciation are best learned by listening. The ear will guide the listener far more effectively and accurately than the written music, transcription of the language, transliteration or phonetic approximation possibly can. Remember, therefore, to use what is on the page as a guide or starting point only and listen, listen, listen.

Khmer: The term *Khmer* refers to the people of Cambodia, or to those who are descended from people whose home was Cambodia. Khmer refers also to the language, the culture, and the traditions of the people of Cambodia and Cambodian refugees and immigrants. In general, we have used Khmer in all cases where people are referred to unless there is the likelihood that other ethnic groups of Cambodian nationality are included in the reference, and Cambodia for political, historic, or geographic references.

Court-Classical: These terms are used separately and simultaneously to refer to the music of the wind and percussion ensemble (*pinn peat*) which has traditionally been used to accompany court dances (all-female dancers), masked plays (all-male dancers), shadow plays, and religious ceremonies.

Vatt: A Buddhist temple or pagoda, *vatt* has often been misspelled as "wat." There is no "w" in the Khmer language.

Romanization of Khmer Words:
A Transcription System

Khmer Sound	English Sound:	As in Khmer word: [translation]

Single-Vowel Sounds   *indicates there is no sound close to Khmer

Khmer Sound	English Sound:	As in Khmer word: [translation]
ap	c*ar*p	*kap* [poem]
ap	j*o*b	*dap* [bottle]
app	c*u*p	*khapp* [thick]
app	t*o*p	*sapp* [corpse]
at	c*ar*t	*kat* [ID card]
at	*ough*t	*that* [drawer]
att	c*u*t	*batt* [lose]
att	l*o*t	*chatt* [bitter]
ay	t*ie*	*bay* [rice]
eh	*ye*s	*seh* [horse]
en	pl*ai*n	*sen* [cent]
en	*	*samnen* [offering]
enn	m*e*n	*chenn* [Chinese]
ey	*	*srey* [female]
ih	p*o*lice	*nih* [this] (aspirated ending)
in	m*ea*n	*masin* [machine]
inn	w*i*n	*minn* [not]
oh	*	*proh* [male]
ok	*	*thok* [cheap]
okk	*	*tokk* [table]
om	*	*krom* [under]
omm	*	*kromm* [group]
or	*	*tror* [fiddle]
orng	*	*korng* [gong]
ut	p*ut*	*chhut* [act]

Double-Vowel Sounds

Khmer Sound	English Sound:	As in Khmer word: [translation]
ai	f*igh*t	*dai* [hand]
aim	s*ome*	*praim* [five]
aing	*	*baraing* [French]
ao	h*ow*	*sao* [Saturday]
au	l*ow*	*dau* [change]
ea	*ear*	*tea* [duck]
eah	*	*Preah* [Buddha]
eak	*	*yeak* [giant]
eo	*	*keo* [glass]
eu	mili*eu*	*chheu* [wood]
ie	id*ea*	*tien* [candle]
oam	w*arm*	*roam* [dance]
oat	*wha*t	*moat* [mouth]
ou	*you*	*krou* [teacher]
uo	*your*	*khuor* [brain]
uoh	*	*puoh* [snake]

<u>Triple-vowel Sounds</u>

eou	*	*peou* [youngest]
oeu	*	*punloeu* [light]
oeung	*	*noeung* [and]

<u>Consonant Sounds</u>

ch	*	*chek* [banana]
chh	*ch*urch	*chhoeu* [sick]
chhng	*	*chhngay* [far]
kh	*c*ake	*khaim* [bite]
khnh	*	*khnhomm* [I]
ng	si*ng*er	*nhuoh* [ogre]
nh	ca*ny*on	*nhaim* [eat]
p	s*p*eak	*pi* [two]
ph	*p*en	*phoum* [village]

NOTE: In most cases the final consonant is not pronounced in Khmer. Rather, many of the words ending in consonants have an aspirated ending.

1
Historical
and Cultural
Background

MAPS

SOUTHEAST ASIA

©1990 World Music Press. (This map may be photo-copied.)

CAMBODIA

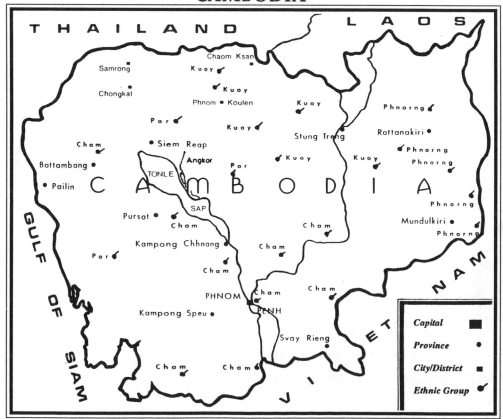

(Map by Sam-Ang Sam. May be photo-copied.)

1 Historical and Cultural Background

As one of the mainland Southeast Asian countries (south of China and east of India), Cambodia is situated in the lower corner of the Indochinese Peninsula. Cambodia is bounded on the west by Thailand, on the north by Thailand and Laos, on the east by Vietnam, and on the south by the Gulf of Siam (see map). At 66,000 square miles, Cambodia is about the size of the state of Washington. Because of its central "crossroads" location in Southeast Asia, Cambodia has been the recipient of considerable foreign influence throughout recorded history.

Geography

Two important geographical features, the Mekong River and the Tonle Sap (Great Lake) have dominated the Cambodian economy and regulated the lives of people for many centuries. The Mekong River traverses the eastern half of Cambodia from north to south. Its total length (from its source in central China) is about 2,600 miles, of which 500 run through Cambodia to the Gulf of Siam (see map). Almost 10% of the country's area is water or marshland, and this area increases during the summer monsoon season when the Tonle Sap, the Mekong and the Bassac rivers overflow their banks and inundate marshes, forests and cultivated fields.

There are sparsely settled hills and plateaus in the northeast. Along the Gulf coast are the heavily-forested Cardamom and Elephant Mountains. The greatest portion of Khmer people live in the central plains, in cities like Phnom Penh, the capital, Siem Reap, Battambang, and Kampong Cham. The centuries-old farm villages along the Mekong and Tonle Sap have grown to the size of cities, with residents still dependent on the resources the waters provide.

Because of the topographical variety, from fertile plains and marshes to forest, bush and mountains, Cambodia is home to abundant plant and animal life. Among the trees found in Cambodia are rubber, palm, cotton, kapok, mango, banana, and orange. Cultivated plants include corn, peppers, tobacco, cotton, sugar, mulberries, and indigo. Betel vines, paddy and lotus grains are also found in profusion. Native bird species include herons, egrets, cranes, pheasants, wild ducks, marabous (a kind of stork with a pouch of pink skin that it distends), pelicans, and cormorants (a kind of seabird commonly used for catching fish, with a long neck, hooked bill and bright distensible skin under the mouth). Hunters find tigers, leopards, panthers, bears and small game, as well as wild elephants, rhinoceroses, wild oxen and buffalo all throughout Cambodia.

Climate

The seasonal monsoons determine rainfall and the temperature of Cambodia. From May until October, the summer monsoon wind brings heavy rainfall and temperatures up to 90-degrees F. During the wet season, there may be more than three feet of rain and floods that raise the water levels of the lakes and rivers to overflowing. From mid-October through April, the dry monsoon wind brings slightly cooler (about 75-degrees F.) and drier weather to the country.

The countryside of Cambodia.

Morning Street Activities, Phnom Penh. (Photo by Yang Sam, 1989.)

Almost 90% of Cambodia's inhabitants still engage in agricultural pursuits. As one of the countries of the Asian "rice bowl," Cambodia produces enough rice to feed its population and to export **Economy** to countries throughout the world. During earlier periods, particularly the Angkor period (802-1432), Cambodia produced not one rice crop per year but four, inspiring the envy of China and the old Chinese phrase, "as wealthy as Cambodia." While there have been many varieties of rice resulting from farmers experimenting, the "sticky" or "wet" rice is best suited for the subtropical lowland environment subject to monsoons.

Second in importance to rice, the fishing industry provides the main source of protein in the diet, and is a boon to the Cambodian economy. During the dry season, the Tonle Sap becomes an extensive fresh water fishing center, the largest in Southeast Asia. Almost all of the 100,000 tons of fish caught is fresh-water carp. The marine fisheries along the Gulf of Siam, although underdeveloped, provide a wide variety of species, including mackerel, jack, drum, snapper, grouper, and mullet.

Other foods in the Cambodian agricultural economy and diet include corn, first introduced by the French as an agricultural product, the indigenous sugar palm (as opposed to cane sugar) which thrives on rich well-drained soil, and pepper, found on the seaward slopes of the Elephant Range, and traditionally tended to by Chinese laborers. While poultry and hogs are raised for domestic consumption, fish rather than meat supplies the most protein by a wide margin.

Since the establishment of the first rubber plantation in 1921, Cambodia has consistently ranked in the top ten among the world's producers of natural rubber. About 55% of the rubber trees are tapped daily, and the contents of the collecting cups are then filtered, developed into smoked or dried sheet, crepe, and latex, and exported to other countries, most notably the United States.

Cambodia's history is long and intricately interwoven with that of the many royal and religious figures who claim places both **History** in folklore and historical documentation. The legends, inscriptions on ancient temples and monuments, fragmented records found in Cambodia, China, India, and much later, France, tell the tale of the Khmer people and the many contenders for the rich and fertile lands of Cambodia. While the Khmer acknowledge the contributions of foreign cultures to their own, they also recognize their distinctive traditions and customs and the rich historical past which shaped them.

Racial migrations into the mainland regions of Southeast Asia occurred in prehistoric times, as early as the Neolithic period. The Khmer, who comprise about 85% of the population of present-day Cambodia, came down from the northwest in about 2,000 B.C. to settle in the fertile Mekong Delta area. Two powerful states had already been established in Cambodia by earlier Indonesian peoples at the time of the Khmer arrival: Champa, the area that is now most of southern Vietnam, and Funan (Founan), the area that covered what is now most of Cambodia and part of central Vietnam. The Funanese people, who lived in the lower Mekong River region, overcame the Chams and the

Khmer and by the fifth century A.D. exercised the rights of overlords in their vast kingdom that stretched as far as the Bay of Bengal, including the Malay Peninsula.

One of the Funan kingdom's vassal states was the Khmer state of Chenla, situated in the region of northern Cambodia and southern Laos. In the sixth century A.D., Chenla overcame Funan and reversed the position of overlord and vassal. During the reign of Isanvarman I, who married a princess of the neighboring kingdom of Champa, Chenla completely absorbed the Funan kingdom and extended the Khmer territory to the Chinese border. The name "Cambodia" was derived from this period, after the founder of the Khmer dynasty, Kambu Svayambhuva or "Kambuja."

The Khmer people regard the Angkor Period (802-1432) as the height of their power and greatness, and a time in which their customs and traditions were spread through much of Laos, Vietnam, Thailand, and the Malay peninsula. The kings Jayavarman II and Jayavarman VII of the period are still hailed as heroes who asserted the independence of the Khmer Empire, developed its economy, built hospitals and temples, and raised the Sanskrit literature to new heights of scholarship. Jayavarman VII was responsible for establishing Buddhism as the state religion, and adapting it to create a Buddah-king cult. The arts flourished. The Angkor Vatt of the period is an archaeological treasure of this brilliant period of Khmer history, a monument to Cambodia's glorious past.

Following the death of Jayavarman VII, the Khmer Empire began to fall apart. The people had been exhausted by the huge construction projects and wars of conquest during the Angkor period. The downfall of Angkor was brought about by the Thai kingdom of Ayuthaya, which finally captured Angkor in 1431. King Ponhear Yat of the vastly reduced Khmer Empire made Phnom Penh his capital, and Angkor was ultimately abandoned to the jungle. For the next four centuries, a subdued Khmer people struggled to maintain a national identity. Much of their former culture was destroyed or lost, including treasures and documents.

Because of the continued aggression by the Siamese of Thailand and Annamese of Vietnam, Cambodia appealed to France for protection in 1863. For nearly a century, the French exploited Cambodia commercially, and demanded political, economic, and social powers. In 1886, along with Vietnam, Laos, and part of South China, Cambodia became part of the Indochinese Union or "French Indochina."

During the second half of the twentieth century, the political situation in Cambodia became chaotic. King Norodom Sihanouk, who had come to the throne in 1941, proclaimed Cambodia's independence from France in 1953. Sihanouk ruled the country struggling to maintain Cambodia's neutrality during the political upheavals in Vietnam and Laos until March 18, 1970, when he was overthrown by troops loyal to the Republic, led by Lon Nol. Just five years later, on April 17, 1975 the genocidal Khmer Rouge led by Pol Pot took over the power and virtually destroyed the lives, health, mentality, morality, education, culture and civilization of the Khmer people. On January 7, 1979, the current government headed by Heng Samrin, chased away the Khmer Rouge with the help of the Vietnamese, and has since controlled Cambodia.

As is typical of so many immigrants to the shores of the United States, the Cambodian refugees fled their homeland in reaction to horrendous events beyond their control. Circumstances were

Exodus from Cambodia

such that it was no longer viable for them to remain in their customary way of life, so hundreds of thousands sought refuge first along the Thai-Cambodian border, and then moved on to other countries: Australia, New Zealand, Japan, France, Switzerland, Belgium, Italy, Canada and the United States. (The United States has granted permanent resettlement to great numbers of Cambodians—more than any other country in the world.) This tremendous Cambodian migration took place in two distinct waves. The first wave, occurring from 1975 until about 1980, involved refugees who by and large were educated and skilled individuals. Since 1980, a second wave brought great numbers of poor and illiterate Cambodians, many of whom suffered traumatic experiences in the process of escape from their homes. This sudden and involuntary plunge into refugee status found many Cambodians practically and psychologically ill-prepared for their wrenching departure from a familiar society and bruising entry into an alien one.

Approximately one quarter of a million Cambodian refugees have come to the United States. They hold a strong belief that America is the land of opportunity, freedom and justice, and view staying behind in Cambodia as a dead-end. Many view life in the United States as a positive orientation into the future, despite the difficult adjustment to a different economic, social and cultural environment. They expect the least and hope for the most.

Younger Cambodian-Americans have limited knowledge of Cambodia and lack the deep sentiment of the older Cambodians. They adjust well to the realities of their new world, and appear convincing in their skill at coping with cross-cultural barriers. Cambodians over the age of fifty often reminisce about their past experiences and customs, and find adjustment and acculturation far more difficult. The language barrier itself slows the process by which they can understand the new American culture. While Cambodian politics and politicians have tended to set people apart by way of various distinctive beliefs, Khmer culture unifies the old and the young, the educated and the illiterate, the rich and the poor. With common language, food, customs, traditions, and religious beliefs, the Cambodians bond together in communities, creating "Cambodian Towns" within cities including Long Beach, California and Lowell, Massachusetts.

In Cambodian communities across America, adults and elders practice religious, national and traditional ceremonies and customs. Although modifications of Cambodia's traditions, they nourish the cultural roots of the older generations (although not always of children and young adults). During major community events such as Ancestral Day and the lunar New Year, Cambodians gather to reaffirm their ethnic solidarity. While the elders long for Cambodia and entertain thoughts of retirement there, younger generations building new lives in the United States are no longer interested in returning to their homeland, and yet are not abandoning their ties to their culture completely, either.

2
Customs
and
Traditions

Angkor Vatt. (Illustration by Yang Sam.)

Jayavarman VII, the last great Cambodian king, who made Buddhism a state religion. (Illustration by Yang Sam.)

Bayan Temple, known also as Angkor Thom, built by Jayavarman VII. Called the Temple of Four Faces. (Illustration by Yang Sam.)

2 Customs and Traditions

The state religion of Cambodia is Theravada Buddhism, a tradition the majority of the population follows. Buddhism constitutes the moral fibre of Khmer lifestyle, and includes tenets of Hinduism and animistic religions as well. Buddhists believe that life is a cycle of death and rebirth in which the individual passes through a succession of incarnations. Depending upon the person's conduct in previous lives, an incarnation may be in a higher or lower status. Buddhists strive to perfect their souls in order to be released from the cycle of death and rebirth and thus enabled to move on to the state of Enlightenment, or nirvana.

Religion

In the traditional Khmer society, boys must enter the monkhood for at least three months during their lifetime, often at the age of twelve or thirteen. During this time, they learn Buddhist philosophy, social morality, and practice praying. The monasteries at which they study are centers of Khmer life, not only for prayer but also for education, medical care, and administrative organization. Since the 1950's, the Buddhist education system has been centered on the transmission of general knowledge of contemporary Khmer culture, from the primary level to the university. The religious institution where Buddhist knowledge could be acquired included the High School of Pali, the Buddhist Institute, and the Buddhist University. The *bonzes* (monks) who reside in these monasteries are at the highest level for achieving nirvana. They wear their distinctive saffron-yellow robes and shaven heads, and set out each morning to collect food from the local people.

The modern Khmer comprise about 85% of the population of Cambodia, and are the products of many centuries of cultural blending. The waves of migrations from India, beginning in the third century B.C., brought about a mixing of ethnic traits for almost a thousand years. The Indo-Malay invasion from Java in the eighth century, A.D., the Thai invasions, and the more recent infusion of Vietnamese, Chinese and Europeans into Cambodia contributed to the composite that is the Khmer ethnic make-up today. The ancestors of many peoples have been assimilated into the culture of Cambodia, and the term "Khmer"—once a description of the dominant ethnic group—now designates nationality. The largest minority groups are the Chinese and the Vietnamese, each constituting about 7%. The remaining minorities include the Khmer Leu, Cham-Malays, Thai and Laotians who have lived side-by-side with the Khmer for centuries, and smaller numbers of recently-arrived Europeans, Japanese, Indians, Pakistanis, and Filipinos.

Ethnic Makeup

The language spoken by the majority people of Cambodia is Khmer. Although there are accents reflecting slight regional variations, it is understood by all people throughout the country.

Language

Unlike Thai, Laotian or Vietnamese, the Khmer language is not tonal. There are borrowed words as well, from the Pali, Sanskrit, and French languages. In particular, the Khmer language has adopted the French words for bread, butter, carrot, coffee, beer, radio, television and other various Western concepts.

The Khmer use a script that is different from the Roman alphabet. The language includes thirty-three consonants, twenty-four vowels, and fifteen full vowels which can be used as a word without having to combine with consonants. However, Khmer is also written from left to right, like English. There is only one form for both singular and plural nouns. For example, the phrase "one pencil" is *khmao dai muoy*; "two pencils" is *khmao dai pi*. The words *khmao dai* ("pencil") are unchanged, whether they are used to refer to one, two or ten. Khmer verbs are not conjugated as they are in English. For example, the Khmer say: *khnhomm teou* ("I go"), *neak teou* ("you go"), *koat teou* ("he/she go [goes]"). *Khnhomm teou sala thngai nih* ("I go to school today"). *Khnhomm teou sala msil minh* ("I go [went] to school yesterday"). (See Romanization guide.)

When speaking Khmer, it is not customary to address someone directly by name. Instead, forms of address such as titles associated with a person's status and age are used, such as big brother, little brother, uncle, aunt, grandpa, and grandma. If a name is used, then the title Mr., Mrs., Miss, or Dr. usually precedes the first name (which comes last in Khmer name-order). For example, a person with the Khmer name of Sok Sambath would appropriately be called Mr. Sambath. (His family name is Sok, his first name is Sambath.)

Khmer forms of address can be very complex. Mastering the intricacies takes much practice over a long period of time, and requires functioning within the actual social context for a speaker to feel fully at ease with them. There are groups and sets of these forms of address, and vocabularies associated with age, status and sex of the persons engaged in conversation. For example, parents use different vocabularies when addressing their children than when addressing their spouse. Children use different vocabularies when addressing each other than when speaking to their parents. Monks have different vocabularies when addressing laymen, and vice versa. The royal language is different from that of common people. The word "sleep" is *phtum* for royalty, *soeung* for monks, *samran* for old people (polite form), *keng* for young people, and *dek* for the common people (which can be impolite and even insulting to some Khmer). The word "yes" is *chah* for royalty and women, *por* for monks, *bat* for men and boys, and *oeu* for older people when addressing the young (which can be impolite and insulting to some young Khmer).

A Khmer household usually consists of a married couple and their unmarried children, although some households include married children and widowed parents as well. Respect for the elders is a part of Khmer culture, but the people of Cambodia rarely emphasize ancestor worship and filial piety to the extent that the Vietnamese and Chinese do. Children are important to the traditional Khmer family, and five children are considered ideal.

Family

A traditional family in Cambodia is an independent unit, sharing domestic, social and religious activities while owning and operating its own rice paddy and vegetable garden. A peasant's house in rural areas may be raised as high as ten feet from the ground on stilts, with a kitchen joined to the house by a ramp. Animals are kept beneath the house. City dwellers with greater wealth may have more space, more privacy, more animals and more furnishings than the average rural household.

In a typical rural setting, the husband is responsible for physically-demanding tasks such as hoeing and preparing the fields for seeding, with husband and wife working together to transplant the rice. The Khmer woman holds a central position in the home, shaping the cultural and ethical development of her children. She is the family treasurer, and stands on an equal footing with her husband. Children have few chores or responsibilities before adolescence, and then are introduced to gender-specific chores such as cooking, sewing and child care for the girls, and farming techniques for the boys.

Clothing

The traditional Khmer outfits are similar to those of the Thai and Laotians. They are the *samput chang kbenn*, or simply, *samput,* a cotton or silk garment of different colors and designs, that is wrapped around the waist with one end rolled and passed between the legs and fastened into a belt at the back; the *sarong*, a cotton or silk single piece of material wrapped around the waist which falls down to the ankles; and the *krama*, a piece of cloth of various sizes made of cotton or silk of different colors, usually with a striped pattern.

In Cambodia, the *krama* is worn by farmers, peasants, and fishermen while working outside. It may be used as a hat to protect a worker's head from the hot sun, wrapped around the forehead and tied at the side or back. This versatile cloth can be twisted into a tight rope, shaped into a circle, and placed on the head like a crown so that big pots or baskets of fruit will balance easily for carrying, and to protect the head from heavy objects. Women often wear the *krama* diagonally across their chest, securing it with a knot or a pin. When going to the river to bathe, men use the *krama* like a wrapped skirt, grabbing the excess and rolling or bundling it at the side.

The *krama* is generally worn as an informal garment. When Khmer people shop, dine, visit, or work in cities they wear western-styled clothes or the *samput*. For special occasions, women might wear the *samput* made of traditional fine Khmer silk.

Festivals

Traditionally, the Khmer celebrate their holidays and festivals year round. Still, they have their favorite calendar days. The most widely celebrated holidays are *chaul chhnaim, phchum benn, bonn phka*, and *bonn cheat*. The *chaul chhnaim* or Khmer New Year takes place from April 13-15 during the dry season, when farmers do not work in the fields. Astrologers determine the actual time and date by calculating the exact moment when the new animal protector (tiger, dragon or snake, for example) arrives. The Khmer in Cambodia spend the entire month in preparation for the celebration, cleaning and decorating their houses with candles, lights, star-shaped lanterns, and flowers. During the first three days of the lunar year, celebrants travel to the pagodas to offer

Buddhist monk dressed in saffron robes. (Illustration by Yang Sam.)

Young dancers rehearse a folk dance during a workshop at Jacob's Pillow. Note the men and women wear the *samput*, fastened in a variety of ways. (Photo by Winnie Lambrecht.)

food to the monks. They pray for prosperity, good health, and show appreciation to their parents and elders. They make resolutions, pay debts, and exchange gifts. Among the many communal experiences of *chaul chhnaim* are participation in music-making, dancing and games, like those you will find in Chapter 4.

Phchum benn is a religious ceremony in September which recalls the spirits of deceased relatives. For fifteen days, people in Khmer villages take turns bringing food to the temples or pagodas. On the fifteenth and final day, everyone dresses in their finest clothes to travel together to the pagodas. Families bring overflowing baskets of food and children offer helpings of the delicacies to the monks. All offer prayers to release the ancestors from sin and to allow them to pass on to a better life. According to Khmer belief, those who do not follow the practices of *phchum benn* receive curses from their angry ancestors.

Bonn phka, the Flower Ceremony, is a fundraising event that is religious in nature. It is organized to raise money to support a local monastery that may seek the building of a new shrine hall or living quarter for the monks. *Bonn phka* is one of the most joyous celebrations for the Khmer, who voluntarily donate money to the event according to their wealth. The *pinn peat* ensemble (featuring xylophones, gongs, shawms, cymbals and drums) performs traditional music, and a drum ensemble called *chhayaim*, whose performers wear comical clown-like masks, enhances the celebration.

Bonn cheat is a national celebration that is political in nature. It is the biggest of all, for it is celebrated as a symbolic gesture of solidarity for the country and nation. Unlike other festivals and celebrations which are community- or village-oriented, this is organized by the government. In Cambodia, from the Monarchy to the Republic and from communism to socialism, the tradition of celebrating the *bonn cheat* has been carried on. The date for the event, however, has changed from one regime to the next. The Monarchy celebrated *bonn cheat* on November 9 (the date of Cambodia's independence from the French), the Republic on October 10 (marking the termination of feudal regime in Cambodia), and the Communist Khmer Rouge on April 17 (the date of their take-over of the Republic and the beginning of the genocidal actions against the population). Today, the socialist government of Cambodia celebrates its *bonn cheat* on January 7, the date when the current regime chased away the dark shadow of the Khmer Rouge and took control of Cambodia.

In the United States, Cambodian refugees continue to celebrate *chaul chhnaim*, *phchum benn*, and *bonn phka* as avenues for continuing their traditional customs, to remember their past experiences, and to add traditional entertainment to their lives. *Bonn cheat* is not celebrated, however, for such celebration is seen as indicative of association, favor, and support for the current or recent regimes in Cambodia.

Birthdays are not important to Khmer people in Cambodia. It is often jokingly explained that "Every time you celebrate your birthday, you are reminded of getting older. If you do not celebrate it, you believe that you are forever young." Nonetheless, many Cambodians in the United States now celebrate their birthdays, with children throwing parties for their parents and parents for their children.

Both in Cambodia and Cambodian communities in the United States, events such as Mother's Day, Father's Day, Valentine's Day, and Wedding anniversaries are not typically celebrated. Instead, a celebration like the Death Anniversary is important, because this is the time for remembering and honoring those relatives and friends who have died.

Traditional Khmer education stresses the transmission of knowledge from teacher to student through the oral process. Teachers lecture to their class, or perform for them, while students take mental and written notes, memorizing ideas for later recall. Teachers are highly respected, and students are expected to regard them as fonts of knowledge. Questioning the teachers can be seen as a challenge, disrespectful, and an insult.

While French terms are still used in Cambodia for the various diplomas and certificates, for official correspondence, and for the signposts of government agencies, English has also been used. The current educational system of the old French colonial programs is somewhat changed today both in content and duration. Primary school education is compulsory for children ages six through ten years. They study mathematics, sciences, Khmer language and literature, social studies, and an assortment of other languages including Spanish, Russian, Vietnamese, French and English. At age eleven, students continue for six years of secondary school education, choosing a major field of study in their final year. For those hoping to enter the university, they must successfully pass the National Baccalaureate II (*Baccalaureat Unique*) examination. The license is the terminal degree offered by most universities in Cambodia. The birth of higher education in Cambodia is relatively recent. The oldest university (Buddhist University) was created in 1954 and the latest (University of Battambang) came into being in 1967. Even during the pre-1975 period, Khmer universities already faced problems of shortages in both native and foreign teachers and teaching materials. Under the control of the Khmer Rouge (1975-1979), all educational institutions were closed, allowing the Khmer people no opportunity for formal education. Today, some universities have been re-opened, but instructional time is shortened due to a severe lack of teachers, and also to provide underpaid teachers with the time to hold a second job to maintain themselves and their families. Even in these difficult circumstances, the Khmer people recognize the absolute importance of education. The Ministry of Education supports and supervises all levels of education today. The state provides expenses for buildings, furniture, teaching equipment, materials and teachers' salaries. There are no fees imposed on students at any level of education. Some universities, including the University of Fine Arts, even provide such services as board and lodging to allow students (especially orphans) to reside on the university compound for easy access to artistic training.

Although they are very much a part of Khmer life, music and the arts have little place in formal education. At the primary and secondary levels, while children may recite poems, learn folk tales, and sing popular songs under the guidance of their classroom teacher, there is no provision within the structure of the formal educational system for the study of the sophisticated vocal or instrumental traditions of Khmer art music. Training is undertaken instead by special arrangements with private teachers outside the schools, or more likely, at the University of Fine Arts with members of the Faculty of Music or the Faculty of Choreographic Arts.

The arts of Cambodia, along with religion, literature, philosophy, and architecture, are almost Indian in inspiration and expression. Many Khmer kings were of Indian descent, and royal courts, temples,

and statuary were modeled on those in India. Early epic literature reveals, by its frequent allusions to Indian literature, a familiarity not only with the standard religious and philosophical works of Hinduism but also with the classic epic poems such as the Ramayana and the Mahabharata. The practice, initiated in the Khmer royal courts, of reciting texts, as well as the major theme used in the Khmer masked play, shadow play, painting and sculpture, did much to increase this familiarity.

A complex folklore has arisen from the blend of beliefs in pagan spirits and in Hindu mythical figures. The fantastic and supernatural have a great appeal to the Khmer and indeed have proven a considerable comfort in times of stress. The misery and fear experienced by the Khmer stimulated their imaginations, and as a result, the legends created have taken root in the Khmer folkways.

The visual and performing arts of the Khmer people, deliberate in pace but infused with spirit, are important aspects of the culture. The history of Cambodia, its society, customs, and beliefs are all expressed through the various art forms. On the old sculptures of the great temple of Ankgor are found both musical instruments and *apsara* (celestial dancer) figures. These *vatt* carvings have immortalized Khmer music and dance forms, and have helped in their continuation.

While music plays a significant role in Khmer culture, it is the court dance that may first come to mind when considering the performing arts of Cambodia. Dancers, who are almost exclusively women, wear costumes of embroidered patterns, elaborate jewelry, and beautifully designed masks and headgear. The costumes, dance movements, and gestures identify different characters such as king, queen, prince, princess, and the demon. Young dancers undergo long and tedious training under a strict discipline, developing the desired curve in the arms, elbows, wrists, fingers and waist. Every gesture that the body makes has its own meaning, either literal or symbolic, that renders the performance of court dance as a highly sophisticated form no less expressively intricate than Western ballet.

(Left) *Apsara*, one of the 1,737 figures carved on Angkor Vatt. (Illus. by Yang Sam.)
(Right) Chan Moly Sam (l.) and Somaly Hay (r.) perform an *apsara* dance. (Photo by Bonnie Periale.)

Other art forms of Cambodia include painting, sculpture, and theater forms based on Reamker, the Khmer form of the Indian epic, the Ramayana. The masked play is a theater and dance form, complete with musical accompaniment. The shadow puppet play involves flat leather puppets that are cut into figures of the king, queen, prince, princess, bird, monkey, giant, and clown, and painted with yellow and black lines. They are designed with many small pinholes punched through the leather, through which light passes, producing shadows of intricate, highly decorative figures. (See illustrations below.) The shadows are cast against a white scrim (translucent screen), by torches or burning coconut shells grouped behind the puppeteers. Puppeteers manipulate these decorated puppets by holding and moving sticks attached to various parts of the puppets' limbs. Before the advent of television and films, the shadow play performance was an all-night entertainment enjoyed by people of all ages. It is only rarely performed in its entirety today.

Leather shadow puppets. Note the pinhole design that allows light to shine through in intricate patterns.

Many of the traditional arts of Cambodia are being replaced by more modern and easily accessible forms of entertainment such as radio, television, cassette tapes, compact discs, films, videotapes, and talk shows. In this new environment, the traditional arts of the Khmer people are, unfortunately, in danger of disappearing. In the next chapter, however, we will see how the musicians and dancers now living in the United States and other countries of the world are experiencing an increasing interest in their art. Through lectures, performances, writing and teaching these living archives of Khmer culture are helping to re-establish, maintain and nourish these age-old traditions. This climate of appreciation and rediscovery might inspire young people to help the roots and branches of Khmer culture flourish in the soil of their new homelands.

3
Khmer Musical Forms, Genres and Instruments

3 Khmer Musical Forms, Genres and Instruments

Music in Historical Perspective

Khmer music is intimately connected to the history and geography of the country. From the earliest times, the Khmer may have had their own local music that grew out of Mon-Khmer musical roots—we see hints of these early traditions preserved in the regional folk styles common today. The *saing* [conch shell] reveals a clear horn-like resonance through its calls, and is used with devotion by the Brahmin at the royal palace to signal the arrival of a sovereign; the *sneng* [horn] is used during elephant hunting expeditions; the *ploy* [mouth organ] is used in the folk dance ensemble of *kangok Posatt* [peacock of Pursat]; and the gong ensemble is used in the folk dance tradition of *kapp krabey phoeuk sra* [buffalo sacrifice] by the Phnorng tribal groups inhabiting the hilly plateau.

During the peak of Khmer civilization, the temple compounds at Angkor were centers of music and dance. Carved on the walls of the *Vatt* are *apsara* [celestial dancer] figures, and various instruments that include the *pinn* [angular harp], *korng vung* [circular frame gong], *sampho* [small barrel drum], *skor yol* [suspended barrel drum], *skor thomm* [large barrel drums], *chhing* [small cymbals], and *sralai* [quadruple-reed shawm]. These instruments were believed to have given birth to the present *pinn peat* [ensemble] which accompanies the court and masked play, shadow play, and religious ceremonies. Among Khmer ensembles, the *pinn peat* is the most resonant reflection of the powerful period of Angkor.

As the Khmer Empire went into decline, its musical and artistic forms were affected. In their place a new style of emotional and melancholic music emerged that incorporated a selection of specific melodies, and even their distinctive modes or pitch patterns. This music, when heard today, offers clear aural reference to Cambodia's decline after the Angkor period. The nineteenth century saw a renaissance of Khmer court (classical) music, and in the twentieth century, the Khmer people took upon themselves the conservation and preservation of traditional arts. Masters were identified, and their practices were carefully emulated and documented.

Musical Characteristics

An initial encounter with traditional music of the Khmer may startle the Western listener, who might find it extremely different from Western style and structure. Unlike the predominance of harmony in the West, Khmer music is linear in character. The texture of Khmer music has been described as polyphonic [many independent melodies], heterophonic [simultaneous variations of a melody], and having polyphonic stratification [many layers of sounds].

Scales

Khmer melodies are based upon two main scales, one pentatonic [five tones] and another heptatonic [seven tones]. The tuning concept and practice of these scales has been an everlasting argument. It has become a cliche that the tuning of all Southeast Asian music is "equidistant," i.e. the interval between every two adjacent pitches in a heptatonic scale is the same. (Technically, 171.4 cents as compared to a Western half-step at 100 cents and whole-step at 200 cents). While this is true in much of the classical music of Thailand, such is not the case in Khmer music. Rather, the tuning system varies from tuner to tuner, from ensemble to ensemble, and from place to place. Musicians at the University of Fine Arts, for example tune their xylophones and gongs differently from musicians in Siem Reap province in northern Cambodia.

Ornamentation

Melodies contain important structural pitches or points which are the skeletal structure of the pieces. If transcribed in Western conventional notation, these important pitches appear after the barlines, and closely correspond to the rhythm cycles of eight, sixteen, or thirty-two beats played by a drum. (See Lesson XI.) Ornamentation or embellishment is a special characteristic of Khmer music. Musicians who have developed a high level of skill and mastery of an instrument will provide intricate ornamentations when performing a piece. These ornamentations will reveal the musician's stature, distinguishing an outstanding performer from a mediocre one. A good performance reflects the musician's knowledge of the piece, the idiomatic performance style of their instruments, as well as their own ability to work creatively and skillfully within the tradition while performing.

Meter

Khmer melodies are often composed in duple or quadruple meter. There is no tempo marking or conducter to lead the ensembles. Instead, each ensemble has a lead instrument to start and end a piece, and the drum and cymbal players set the tempo. Rhythmically, Khmer music bears a noticeable kind of "dotted" or uneven rhythm. This is one quality that distinguishes it from the more even rhythm of Thai music.

Categories

Khmer musical pieces are grouped into several categories according to their nature—narrative, descriptive, and sentimental— and also their language, dialect, or regional/national "accents"— Khmer, Laotian, Burmese, Javanese, Chinese, Mon, and European. (Because their names relate to specific groups, their compositions have a certain character, style, and general manner appropriate to each.) These categories are often obvious in the titles, such as "Khyall Bakk Cheung Phnum" [The Wind Blows at the Foot of the Mountain], "Krapeu Kantuy Veng" [Long-Tailed Crocodile], "Sdech Sok" [Sad King], "Khmer Krang Phka" [Khmer String Flowers], "Lao Doeur Prey" [Laotians Walk in the Forest], "Chenn Se" [Chinese Medical Doctor], "Phoumea Doeur Yoeut" [Burmese Walk Slowly], and "Baraing Bakk Phlett" [French Fan].

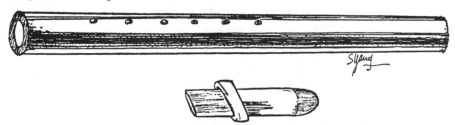

Pey Praboh: double-reed pipe. (Illustration by Yang Sam.)

Musical Instruments

Khmer music is generally assumed to belong to the "gong-chime" culture, in that foremost among its instruments are many types of gongs, xylophones, and metallophones. A variety of aerophones, chordophones, idiophones, and membranophones exist; only the principal ones are described here. Photographs and illustrations of them are grouped in this chapter and also sprinkled throughout the balance of the book.

Aerophones

Khmer aerophones include conch shells, buffalo horns, flutes, free-reeds, double reeds, and quadruple reeds. Of these, the quadruple-reed instrument called the *sralai* is one of the most unique instruments in the world. It consists of a thirteen- to sixteen-inch body of hard wood or ivory with a shape that bulges at the center and flares outward at both ends. Six fingerholes are bored into the center bulge, drilled through sixteen carved pairs of decorative rings which also serve to deter the fingers from slipping in performance. The quadruple-reed (made of four little tongues of dried palm leaf fastened to a brass tube with thread) is placed completely in the mouth, with the performer's lips resting against the *sralai*, and the tongue placed right under the reed to control the opening. If more of the tongue is pressed under the bottom part of the reed and the pressure is slightly increased, the pitch is raised. It is played using only the three middle fingers of each hand. Two sizes of *sralai* exist, each with a two-octave range, and one tuned about a perfect fourth higher than the other.

The Khmer flute, called *khloy*, is of the end-blown duct or fipple variety. It is one of the most popular instruments in Cambodia, partly due to the accessibility of bamboo which is most commonly used to make flutes. Under a straw hut in the fields or on the back of a buffalo, a young boy commonly adds the sound of his *khloy* to the sound of the wind blowing while he watches his cattle. The body of the *khloy* is made of bamboo, wood, metal, or even plastic. There are six or seven fingerholes and a thumbhole (although some do not have this hole). Some also have a membrane hole which is covered by a thin rice paper or bamboo skin to create a buzzing sound quality. The *khloy* has a two-octave range, from approximately D4 (D just above middle C) to D6 (D two octaves higher). Besides its common use as a solo instrument, the *khloy* is also found in the *mohori* [entertainment] and *kar* [wedding] ensembles.

Another important aerophone is the side-blown single free-reed pipe known as *pey pork*. The body of the *pey pork* is made of bamboo or cane with seven fingerholes and one thumbhole. The reed is made of bronze and is placed in a hole approximately one inch from the end of the pipe. The range of the *pey pork* is just over an octave; this is the smallest range of all Khmer wind instruments with the exception of the *sneng* [buffalo horn], which has the range of only a perfect fourth. At one time, the *pey pork* was played to put a medium into a trance or in conjunction with worship of the spirit, and in wedding ensembles. Today, this free-reed pipe is played as a solo instrument or to accompany singing.

The audience listening to these instruments will detect no break in the sounds that might indicate a breath had been taken. This is due to the extremely important technique of **circular breathing** employed by *sralai, khloy* and *pey pork* players. The key to the technique is that about half to two-thirds of the way before the breath is fully used up,

41

the performer expands the cheeks (serving as an air chamber) and pushes the remaining air out through the mouth and into the instrument while taking a new breath through the nostrils. This breath-taking must be done quickly so as to keep the air flowing continuously. To learn the technique, students practice by blowing through a thin soda straw (or in Cambodia, a water lily stalk) into a glass of water to make bubbles. During practice, bubbles must continue without interruption. If the bubbles stop, there has been a break in the flow of air into the water, indicating the circular breathing technique has not yet been mastered.

Common Aerophones

sralai	Quadruple-reed shawm; hardwood or ivory
khloy	End-blown flute; bamboo
pey pork	Side-blown single free-reed pipe; bamboo or cane
pey praboh	Double-reed pipe

Sralai, quadruple-reed shawm. (Illustration by Yang Sam.)

Idiophones

Among the many idiophones of Khmer music are the xylophones, the gongs, and the small cymbals. Khmer xylophones are called **roneat,** and are classified as "bar idiophones." The *roneat* have bamboo or wooden keys which are strung together with two cords running through holes in each key, and are suspended on hooks at each end. The xylophone keys are tuned to desired pitches using tuning blobs called *pramor*, a mixture of lead, beeswax and rosin. The *roneat* player strikes the keys with two mallets having soft or hard heads, for indoor or outdoor performances respectively. Two sizes of *roneat* exist, one with sixteen keys, and another with twenty-one. The *roneat ek* (higher pitched xylophone) is considered to be lead instrument in an ensemble, because of its role in starting a piece or cuing other instruments. The *roneat ek* generally plays variations of a melody that is usually sounded by a vocalist or *sralai* player. Stylistically, the *roneat ek* plays in octaves or less commonly in fourths or fifths.

Another principal instrument of Khmer music is the **korng vung**, a set of sixteen bowl-shaped gongs in a circular frame, used in the *pinn peat* ensemble. The individual gongs that make up the set are made from copper (for bright sound) mixed with bronze (for long life), and are bossed (have a raised section). The gongs are various sizes, and are placed over a rattan frame twelve inches high or so, constructed in the shape of nearly a full circle. Each gong has four holes, two on each side. Gut strings are placed through these holes, then run over the frame and tied to the frame itself. The gongs are suspended

Phon Bin demonstrating *roneat ek* [high-pitched xylophone]. Note mallets tied together with string—a technique common among beginners to maintain the correct distance between mallets for the octave or certain desired intervals. (Photo by Winnie Lambrecht.)

Sam-Ang Sam playing an elaborately decorated *khloy*. (Photo by Bonnie Periale.)

Phon Bin playing the *krapeu*. The *khimm* is in front. (Photo by Winnie Lambrecht.)

Phon Bin demonstrating the *khimm*, hammered dulcimer. (Photo by Winnie Lambrecht.)

Thaun-rumanea drum pair. (Photo by Sam-Ang Sam.)

Sampho (small barrel drum.) (Photo by Sam-Ang Sam.)

Skor arakk (goblet drum). (Photo by Sam-Ang Sam.)

Chhing (small cymbals). (Photo by Sam-Ang Sam.)

Roneat thung (low-pitched xylophone).
(Photo by Sam-Ang Sam.)

Korng thomm (low-pitched circular gongs).
(Photo by Sam-Ang Sam.)

Pinn peat ensemble. Two large barrel drums on the right are *skor thomm*, the *krapeu* is in front. Player to the far left shows position for sitting within the *korng tauch* or *korng thomm*. (Photo by Frank Proschan.)

44

in the frame, arranged so that the largest and lowest-pitched is to the left of the player, the highest is to the right. The player sits in the middle of the set. Each gong is tuned to required pitch using the same *pramor* mixture described above. Soft mallets are used for indoor use, hard ones for outdoor performances.

A critically important instrument in Khmer music is the **chhing,** a pair of bowl-shaped cymbals of thick and heavy bronze, with a small rim. *Chhing* are the timekeeper of the ensemble. They measure about two inches and are joined together with a cord which passes through a small hole at the apex of each one of them. Each cymbal of the pair is held in one hand and the two are struck together. *Chhing* produce open (ringing) and closed (dampened) sounds, called "chhing" and "chhepp." They are marked respectively with the signs (o) for open and (+) for dampened.

Common Idiophones	
roneat	xylophone; suspended bamboo or wooden keys
roneat ek	higher pitched xylophone
roneat thung	lower pitched xylophone
korng vung	set of 16 circular copper/bronze gongs in rack
korng tauch	high-pitched circular frame gongs
korng thomm	low-pitched circular frame gongs
chhing	small bronze cymbals

Membranophones

The *sampho* is considered to be among the most important Khmer musical instruments. The *sampho* is a small barrel drum. Its body is made of hollowed wood, and at either end is a calf-skin head tightened with gut; the center of each head is painted black. The player hits both heads of the *sampho* using his hands. One head is larger than the other, so that the drum produces a lower and a higher tone at each head. They are tuned with a pasty mixture of cooked rice and ashes from burnt branches of the coconut tree. The *sampho* controls the tempo and regulates the rhythmic cycles of Khmer music.

Another membranophone is the set of two drums called the **thaun-rumanea,** which can be found in the *mohori* ensemble. The *thaun* is a goblet-shaped drum, made of a clay or wood body in various sizes. Snake, goat, or ox skin is stretched over the head and then tied to the body with nylon string or wire. The *rumanea* is a flat frame drum similar to the Laotian and Thai *ramana*, Indian *kanjira*, West African and Native American square or circular frame drums, or Irish *bodhran*. The *rumanea* is never played alone, but the *thaun* is occasionally used by itself in the *laim thaun,* a popular music ensemble still heard in the countryside where electric guitars (and electricity) are not available. The drummer uses bare hands to play the *thaun-rumanea.* Cambodian musicians have prescribed three different rhythmic patterns called *muoy choan* [level one], *pi choan* [level two], and *bey choan* [level three] for *thaun-rumanea.* The rhythmic patterns increase in tempo and complexity, from eight beats at the first level, to a doubling to sixteen beats at the second level, and to a quadrupling to thirty-two beats at the third level. The density of the second level is usually greater than the first, and the third level is more dense than the second. (See Lesson XI.)

45

Common Membranophones

sampho	barrel-shaped drum; wood body; 2 calf-skin heads
thaun	goblet-shaped drum; clay or wood body; snake-, goat- or ox-skin head
rumanea	flat frame drum
skor arakk	goblet drum
skor thomm	large double-headed barrel drums

Chordophones

A number of important chordophones are integral to traditional Khmer music. The **tror** is a bowed lute, once considered a folk fiddle. It is believed to be a modification of the Chinese *erh-hu*, which was used in the Chinese ensemble brought to Cambodia around the turn of the century. The *tror* has a range of approximately one octave. There are five types of *tror*: *tror chhe* (high-pitched two-stringed fiddle), *tror so tauch* (medium-high-pitched two-stringed fiddle), *tror so thomm* (medium-low-pitched two-stringed fiddle), *tror ou* (low-pitched two-stringed fiddle), and *tror Khmer* (three-stringed spike fiddle). The variety of *tror* are used in the *arakk* [worship of the spirit], the *kar*, and *mohori* ensembles. They are also heard as accompaniment to vocal music.

The **khimm** is a chordophone instrument belonging to the board zither family. Today board zithers can be found in many places under different names such as *santir* (Iran and Iraq), *chang* (Soviet Union), *santoor* (India), *yangum* (Korea), *hackbrett* (Switzerland), *yang chin* (China), *cimbalom* (Hungary), *kim* (Thailand), *dan tam thap luc* (Vietnam) and hammered dulcimer (North America). The Khmer *khimm* may have been brought to Cambodia at some time during this century, along with the Chinese opera, which has since been modified and adapted to a local form of theater called *basakk*. There are two sizes of *khimm*, both of which have fourteen fixed bridges, over which run double and triple metal strings of two and one-half octaves. They are played with a pair of padded sticks. The *khimm* is prominent not only in the *basakk* ensemble but also in the *mohori* ensemble that accompanies Cambodian folk dances and plays.

Still another important Khmer chordophone is the **krapeu**, a long three-stringed zither. A similar instrument, *jakay*, can be found in Laos and Thailand, and in Burma where it is called *mi gyaun*. *Krapeu* means crocodile. The instrument received its name because its body or board resonator has the shape of a crocodile. Twelve frets are mounted on the body of the instrument, and two nylon strings play melody while one metal string sounds a drone. The *krapeu* player uses a small piece of buffalo horn or ivory as a plectrum or pick, which is tied to the player's index finger with a string. Several ensembles, including the *kar*, *mohori*, and *ayai* [alternate singing], feature the *krapeu*.

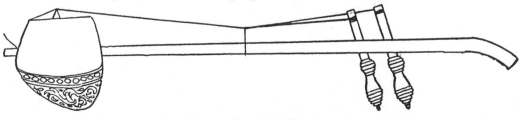

Tror ou (low-pitched two-stringed fiddle). Illustration by Yang Sam.

46

Common Chordophones

tror chhe	high-pitched two-stringed fiddle
tror so tauch	medium-high-pitched two-stringed fiddle
tror so thomm	medium-low-pitched two-stringed fiddle
tror ou	low-pitched two-stringed fiddle
tror Khmer	three-stringed spike fiddle
khimm	hammered dulcimer with 14 bridges
krapeu	long three-stringed zither, 12 bridges; played with a plectrum

Phon Bin, instrument builder and musician living in Massachusetts, demonstrating *tror Khmer*. (Photo by Winnie Lambrecht.)

A *tror so tauch* player at the Lowell, Mass. Folk Festival, 1988. (Photo by Winnie Lambrecht.)

Phon Bin demonstrating the unusual *chapey dang veng* [long-necked lute]. A *roneat ek* is in the background. (Photo by Winnie Lambrecht.)

Musical Forms and Genres

Among the most important Khmer musical forms is the dance music of court and folk settings and occasions. Khmer court dance has been associated with the court of Cambodia for over a thousand years, at least since the time of the Angkor period. Likewise, folk dance has been close to the heart of rural life in Cambodia from time immemorial.

In the Angkor Vatt compound, gigantic bas-relief master-pieces symbolize the union of celestial and earthly beings in the court dances that were offered to the god-king during the golden

Court Dance

age of the Khmer culture. Following the wars with Thailand, a renaissance of Khmer culture occurred that included the restoration of the court dance. Female dancers were preferred for court dances, with male dancers reserved for the role of the monkey in the dance drama, and for the performance of masked plays.

Court dancers were trained from childhood in the royal palace. They seldom left the palace grounds, unless to attend to the king in his travels. Dancers were trained from the age of five or six for a repertoire that included pure dance pieces, and dance dramas based upon romantic and mythological stories as well as the great epics such as *Reamker* (the Indian epic, the Ramayana), *Preah Chinavung*, and *Preah Chann Korup*. Young girls underwent strenuous training, perfecting the gestures that involved their arms, elbows, hands wrists, legs and feet. Early-morning training sessions began with an intense routine of bending and stretching the limits by which the body can naturally be extended, twisted and turned.

Costumes of Khmer court dance include intricate masks and headdresses (called *mkott*), and elaborate jewelry worn on the neck, forearms, wrists, and ankles. The jewelry is made of precious stones, gold, silver, and brass, depending upon the patronage of the troupe. The court dances added lustre and grace to the king's courts, in particular during the king's anniversaries, religious and ceremonial festivals, national ceremonies, and in the entertainment of the king's guests

Muni Mekhala Dance Drama featuring Chan Moly Sam (l.), and Somaly Hay (r.) in the role of Ream Eyso the giant or ogre. (Photo by Bonnie Periale.)

48

(Above) Court dance hand gesture meaning "flower." There is a series of stylized gestures with specific interpretive meanings. (Photo by Bonnie Periale.)

(Left) Chan Moly Sam wearing elaborate *mkott* [crown] for court dance. These crowns and other jewelry can be very heavy. (Photo by Bonnie Periale.)

Robaim nesat [trap-fishing dance]. A folk dance. (Illustration by Yang Sam.)

Folk dances of Cambodia and their musical accompaniment are performed by and for the people of rural areas. Adults and children alike dance to increase a communal sense of security, to release emotions, to communicate with their ancestors, and to bring good fortune to the community. Especially for religious ceremonies, traditional festivities like the rituals of harvest season, and recreational gatherings, folk dances based on local legends and on the life of the people in the villages are performed, improvised, and injected with new gestures. While court dances are restricted to their classical form with a prescribed language of movement and gesture, folk dance is a reflection of the feelings of rural people and their spontaneous response to the music at hand.

Folk Dance

Robaim chraut srauv [harvest dance]. (Illustration by Yang Sam.)

Because the Khmer value music in their lives, it is heard on the occasions of a baby's birth, at funerals, at hairshaving events, and even in the boxing arena. Boxers do not fight without music. In Cambodia, the boxing ensemble consists of one *sralai* (quadruple-reed shawm) and one *sampho* (small barrel drum). Boxing music is unique. There is one piece that is immediately recognized by every Khmer who assists or attends boxing events. This piece is divided into two parts: the invocation of the spirits or *krou* [teachers] to concentrate the boxers' mind and to give them confidence, and the fight itself. Music for the first part is slow and in a rubato (free and flexible rhythm) style; the *sralai* plays the melody accompanied by the *sampho* which provides only a few strokes at important structural points in the melody. The second part is in a steady and faster tempo than the first. As the boxing rounds progress, the music accelerates and stops only at the end of the rounds or when a boxer is knocked out. In a good fight, the audience also joins by clapping their hands in rhythm with the *sampho*. (See Lesson XII.)

Boxing Music

The Khmer wedding has traditionally been a prominent occasion for music, and *phleng kar* [wedding music] developed over the centuries as one of Cambodia's most popular musics. *Phleng kar* refers to the ensemble, one of the oldest in Cambodia, and also to the repertoire. Instrumentation includes a low- and hi-pitched *tror*, *khloy*, *krapeu*, *khimm*, a goblet drum called *skor arakk*, and a singer. The fixed airs of the *phleng kar* can be modified to suit the social rank of the couple and their family. The *phleng kar* ensemble plays throughout various events of a wedding ceremony that lasts three days and three nights. Each part of the ceremony is accompanied by the ensemble, from the time of building a house as a dowry to the ceremony of the cutting of the hair of the bride and groom, to the rite of *sampeah neak ta* [Salute to the Local Guardian Spirit], during which cotton threads are tied to the wrists of the married couple. Because marriage is so common, in Cambodia and even in the United States *phleng kar* music remains popular.

Traditional wedding 1989, Danbury, Connecticut. The bride and groom take part in the rite of *sampeah neak ta* [salute to the local guardian spirit] during which cotton threads are tied to the wrists of the couple by many of the guests. (Photo by Tho Sangphet.)

These musicians were brought in from New York City for the wedding in Danbury, Connecticut. (Photo by Tho Sangphet.)

51

Tradition and Change

The Communist, genocidal regime of Pol Pot claimed the lives of millions of Khmer adults and children. Musicians, dancers and other artists were not exempted. So many lost their lives that the method by which traditional musical skills and repertoire had always been transmitted was virtually destroyed. The present condition that exists in refugee camps and in Khmer communities in adopted countries abroad, including the United States, is, sadly, a confusing one. The lack of a clear path to solid musical expertise and in-depth knowledge has actually endangered the preservation of many musical styles, techniques, and pieces. Some musicians who learned their art in refugee camps are not aware of—or do not pay attention to—issues of authenticity, preservation and tradition. In addition, because so many of the highly trained musicians died, the neophytes have virtually no way to be exposed to the original versions for much of their repertoire, and thus pieces and techniques have changed without the performers fully realizing where the changes were made. Instead, they apply a personal and popular interpretation to what had always been sophisticated forms and styles.

There are now only a few artists teaching and performing who were formally charged with carrying on the tradition closely. The resulting break in the oral tradition has resulted in the loss of more than half of the oldest melodies that had previously been passed on from generation to generation. Now many pieces are totally unknown, while others are known only by name. Many musicians find the demands of making a living in the modern world leave little time for serious practice, and because there is frequently little monetary compensation for performances, most musicians must treat music as a hobby. The result is that when certain music is needed for particular celebrations there is no time for adequate rehearsal, and both skill and accuracy suffer.

In particular, the following developments in traditional music and dance have been observed in Cambodian settlements in the United States, the Thai border camps, in France and in Cambodia itself.

1. Because of the lack of musicians and instruments, the *pinn peat* ensemble which was traditionally comprised of *roneat* (xylophone), *korng vung* (circular frame gongs), now also includes *tror* (two-stringed fiddle), *krapeu* (three-stringed zither), *khimm* (hammered dulcimer), and *khloy* (duct flute). Some of these modified *pinn peat* ensembles use Western flute instead of the *khloy*.

2. Because of the lack of *sralai* (quadrulple-reed shawm) players, the *pinn peat* ensemble uses a *roneat ek* (high-pitched xylophone) to play the traditional and well-known *saloma* piece, which had always been played on a *sralai*.

3. Because of the lack of *skor thomm* (large double-headed barrel drums), the *sampho* (small double-headed barrel drum) player now plays both parts on the *sampho* only. The result is a decline in timbral variety.

4. Because of the lack of female dancers who traditionally perform male and giant roles in the *lkhon kbach* (court dance), male dancers are now employed for those parts.

5. Because of the inadequate knowledge of the repertoires of both music and dance, substitutions and abbreviations of classical pieces have occurred. For example, some musicians cannot play the two or three sections of a standard traditional piece, and repeat the first section two or three times instead.

Today, traditional Khmer music is performed in Cambodia and ## Khmer Music
in the Cambodian communities around the world for such occasions ## in the U.S.
as weddings, religious ceremonies in the temples, and during dance
and theater performances. Of the approximately one quarter of a million Cambodian refugees resettled in the United States, about three dozen pricipal musicians and dancers are actively performing for audiences in North America, in dance and music residencies in schools, universities, and museums, as well as for celebrations within Cambodian communities. Musicians actively performing include Bun Loeung (MN), Chhoeuy Man (CA), Chum Ngek (MD), Dip Seth (CA), Dul Chea (CA), Heam Yoeung (WA), Iv Sary (CA), Khlay Ra (MD), Kim Chhay (MA), Kong Peang (PA), Pel Sam-Uon (WA), Phan Bin (MA), Poeung Noeung (WA), Pok Chhum (CA), Sam Sam-Ang (WA), So Vann (WA), Sou Hoeurn (WA), To Hear (CT), Ung Chinary (AZ), Van Pok (PA), Van Yan (PA), and Yin Ponn (CA). Principal dancers include Chhim Chan Dara (CA), Hay Somaly (CT), Hing Rachana (MN), Meas Massady (MD), Hing Thavaro (MN), Moeur Sokhanarith (CT), Nuth Vanthy (MN), Phoung Phan (CT), Sam Chan Moly (WA), Sin Ny (MD), Tes Sam-Oeun (MD), and Yim Devi (VA). (Note: These names have been listed here using the traditional style of name order.)

For practical and economic reasons, folk music is more often heard than other Khmer genres because it is used at wedding ceremonies which occur weekly in Cambodian communities across the country. Musicians are paid when playing for these ceremonies. The court (classical) music, unfortunately, is of serious concern. Because it accompanies the infrequent or annual-only performances of court dance (during the Cambodian New Year), it is becoming an endangered musical species.

Young Khmer people often find their parents and older relatives conservative, old-fashioned, and backward. They perceive Khmer music, songs and dances as too slow and therefore boring. Unfortunately, there have been few young Khmer seeking out lessons on traditional instruments, or who are learning to perform Khmer songs. Still, many will attend concerts of the traditional music and dance.

The dance traditions seem to be faring a bit better at this point. Both folk and court traditions of the dance are well-preserved, as there are dancers who seem to want to learn and perform both traditions. Seeing the need to pass on Khmer traditional culture to the younger generation, and recognizing young people's enthusiasm for learning the dance, Cambodian associations in several communities (for example, the Cambodian-American Heritage in Maryland and the Cambodian Studies Center in Washington) offer classes in the traditional choreographic arts. In addition, community arts and outreach groups such as Country Roads: Refugee Arts Group in Boston, and the Jacob's Pillow Dance Festival in Massachusetts are actively seeking and working with Cambodian dancers and musicians to offer master classes, document traditional pieces on film, and sponsor concerts and festivals.

Rock music was enjoyed in Cambodia by the young Khmer even before the war. Khmer popular music, once called *phleng Manil* [Manila music], is probably fifty years old, and was believed to be brought to Cambodia by the Filipinos in the 1940's. When compared to American rock music, the Khmer version seems simple and old-fashioned. When it began to emerge, Khmer rock music incorporated Latin American rhythms such as the bolero, the cha-cha, the tango, and the bossanova into its repertoire. Because Khmer rock bands today play for older as well as younger listeners, the Latin American rhythms are still popular. Moreover, as Khmer rock musicians are not as dedicated as some Americans who earn their living as members of professional bands, Khmer rock music tends to retain its simpler and earlier flavor.

While using the borrowed rhythms from the West, Khmer rock musicians also include their traditional Khmer rhythms—*roam vung, roam kbach, saravann,* and *laim leav*— in their rhythmic repertoire necessary for the social gatherings or parties which involve social dancing. What makes this rock music distinctly Khmer is the playing style, the incorporation of Khmer rhythms, and the use of traditional Khmer melodies. Of particular note is the fact that among the various Khmer genres, rock music is the most popular, because it is appreciated by young Khmer who are willing to pay for this kind of entertainment. In the Khmer music industry, consequently, Khmer rock or pop music is in greatest demand and is easily available for purchase from Asian stores in Cambodian, Vietnamese and Chinese communities where there are large concentrations of Asian refugees and immigrants.

Laim leav dance - a popular dance and rhythm.

54

Teaching and Learning

Teaching and learning Khmer music is a practical and performance-oriented process. Cambodian musicians tend not to be theorists; they do not verbalize about their music. Likewise, intelligent listeners judge musicians by their playing rather than their discourse about music. Those who master the art of Khmer court music do so by developing their listening ear and their creative mind for the embellishment which is the ultimate in Khmer musical expression.

In the tradition of becoming a Khmer musician, every student must experience an apprenticeship that involves several years and stages. Musical training comprises long-standing Khmer rituals that begin with the taking of a teacher. A student is introduced to a teacher by a third person, who may be another teacher, a relative, or a friend. As a social acquaintance is established, the student can prove his commitment, courtesy, respect and patience to the future teacher. Should the teacher accept him, a ceremony called *sampeah krou* [salute the teacher] is prepared for the student, in which permission and blessing from the teacher's teachers is requested. The ceremony includes an offering of five incense sticks, five candles, five meters of cloth, and five *riels* (in the old days, five *riels* could buy a bowl of noodles and a cup of coffee). During the course of study, the student often brings gifts for the teacher: money, fruits, cakes, and cigarettes. The student continues to show respect and obedience to the teacher in order to assure a warm atmosphere and emotional harmony. The relationship is very much a mentorship, and not simply a situation of "taking lessons."

Musical knowledge is traditionally passed on orally from master teacher to student, without the use of notation. The student imitates and follows the master during private lessons. The teacher plays a phrase on an instrument, and the student repeats. Again the teacher plays a phrase, and again the student repeats it. When the first phrase is memorized, the modeling-and-imitation process is applied to a second phrase, a third phrase, and so on, until the piece has been memorized. With the learning of each new phrase, there is the task of linking it in performance to the earlier phrases. Through this process, Khmer musicians learn a repertoire of several hundred pieces by heart.

Since the introduction of Western music to Cambodia, musical notation has been used by teachers and students at the University of Fine Arts in Phnom Penh. Notation can expedite teaching and learning, but it can also prove to be a disadvantage if musicians become dependent on notation rather than on their own ears and intellects. Notation is best used by students who write only the fundamental melody and important structural pitches of a piece, master and memorize these melodies, and then discard the transcriptions. In actual performance, students develop the skill to provide variation, ornamentation, and embellishment appropriate to the style. It is through many years of listening to their teachers that students learn to master the complexities of traditional Khmer music.

Staging the Shadow Play. (Illustration by Yang Sam.)

4

A Guide
to the Music of
Cambodia

4 A Guide to the Music of Cambodia

The selections which follow are designed as an introduction to the traditional music and culture of Cambodia, to be used by groups with the guidance of an instructor or by individuals working independently with the tape and book. Teachers of music, social studies and language arts, general classroom teachers, and community outreach leaders may find effective use of the lessons, and both Khmer and non-Khmer readers and listeners will find the recorded selections and annotation enlightening and enjoyable. The written annotation to the taped musical selections unravels the intricacies of Khmer music, and presents the songs in cultural context that encompasses information on geography, language and literature, folklore and customs. The "Study Guide" for each selection is oriented toward participatory experiences, with provision allotted for the development of listening skills, critical thinking about Khmer music, the related arts and their context within the culture. Each "Study Guide" has a separate section entitled "For the Music Professional" (intended for music teachers, ethnomusicologists or the serious student) that offers more detailed musical analysis, additional experiences in rhythmic responses, the singing voice, and instrumental performance.

This collection presents a varied sampling of treasures from the venerable Khmer culture representing folk and game songs, instrumental selections, and stories. The fourteen lessons which follow are logically sequenced to facilitate an understanding of Khmer music and culture. Each piece corresponds to a recorded selection, found in the same order on the companion tape. Traditional and composed songs are notated, and each is presented with its text and literal translation. (Please refer to the "Notes" section at the beginning of this book for general information about the transcriptions.) The cultural context of the game songs, wedding songs, dance music, instrumental pieces, and musical stories is presented, so that the music can more easily be perceived as it is intended—a reflection of the traditions which Khmer hold dear. To that end, each selection opens with a personal comment or anecdote by Sam-Ang.

The study guides offer step-by-step procedures, so that the user can recognize the intent of the lessons to develop both musical skills and cultural understanding. Still, the lessons may provide only a framework for the creative teacher, student, or independent reader-listener, who will identify the critical content and tailor it to suit classroom or individual needs. Each section may be presented as a self-contained unit, or may be expanded or abbreviated as necessary. We have suggested age and grade levels. Feel free to make adjustments to allow the widest use of the material in a variety of settings. We have included suggestions for further discussion of cultural issues, and ideas for further musical experiences that include listening, singing, movement and instrumental performance.

While there are highly sophisticated musical traditions, genres and performance practices within Khmer culture that demand a lifetime of training, even beginners can know the enriching experience of singing a traditional Khmer song, playing a traditional Khmer melody on flute, recorder or xylophone, or moving with stylized gestures in response to popular Khmer music. Careful, repeated listening to the companion tape will reveal the delicate, refreshing beauty of much of the music, and also the stylistic nuances typical of performances of even the most modern popular songs and melodies.

The music of Cambodia can be presented for its sound essence alone, a kind of sonic artifact of the culture, but a broader study of Khmer culture will lead to a fuller understanding of musical—and artistic—traditions. An immersion into the world of Cambodia and Cambodian-Americans may entail the use of maps and photographs of the cities and countryside of Cambodia and the Khmer people. We have provided numerous drawings and photographs. Refer to the selected bibliography, discography and filmography for resources for stories, slides, and videotapes to add a broad cultural context for experiencing the music.

Invite Khmer residents from the local community to visit the group to share their past experiences and customs, to tell a story, to show samples of traditional clothing or art, to play a game or sing a song, help with pronunciation, share a recipe or play an instrument. Such a guest will lend a humanistic real-life perspective to the study of both the music and culture, and will be heartened by the interest taken in the gift of their knowledge.

For the Music Professional

At the end of each "Study Guide" is a special section of particular interest to music teachers, ethnomusicologists and serious students. This special focus includes additional information on the musical structure or techniques, and more in-depth activities specifically related to musical understanding and performance of the selections. For singing in Khmer style, listeners should recognize that vibrato is not a part of the performance style. Both children and adults tend to employ the light "head voice" rather than the heavier "chest voice"; the emphatic or strident "playground" and "street" voices are not appropriate in this vocal tradition. The pieces have been notated in a fundamental, skeletal approach, and the astute listener will recognize that Khmer melodies are embellished with slides between pitches, passing tones, and occasional turns or trills. (Furthermore, as we described in the "Notes" section at the beggining of the book, there is a problem with transcribing the music to match the pitch of the instruments on the recording. You may have an accurate transcription, but those instruments are not in tune with piano, recorder, flute, xylophone or Orff Schulwerk barred instruments, and an accurate transcription requires several sharps or flats, making it difficult for younger students to read, or impossible for some instruments to play. We have therefore provided transcriptions in the key closest to the actual that will still enable performance on Western or classroom instruments, and in an appendix at the back is an additional transcription in the key of actual taped performance. See also the "Romanization of Khmer Words" guide for some pronunciation assistance. There are many sounds that are impossible to write, however, so once again it is essential to listen to the singers attentively.) To approach the actual Khmer playing and singing style more closely, we invite you to play the tape repeatedly. Listen carefully, and sing along with the performers, polishing and adjusting as you go. If you have a variable speed tape player, increase the speed so that the pitch is raised the half-step to the transcription, and then you may play along as well.

60

Several melodies are presented for performance on classroom instruments such as xylophones and recorders. Unlike many other musical traditions which may be inappropriately "arranged" for easily accessible instruments, some of the music of Cambodia can be authentically reproduced on these instruments since *roneat* (xylophone) and *khloy* (flute) are so central to court (classical) and folk traditions. In particular, the xylophones can present a rewarding experience as a hands-on introduction to Khmer music. Because the tuning system in Cambodia is similar to Western turning (especially in court music), there is no need to "tune" the xylophones as is the case when striving for an authentic tuning of a classroom-simulated Indonesian gamelan or African xylophone ensemble.

Performance Considerations When Using Classroom Instruments

For music and classroom teachers who wish to use xylophones from the Orff instrumentarium, several issues concerning adaptation should be considered. First, metallophones may also be employed to play pieces designated for xylophones, as the gamut of musical instruments in Cambodia includes barred instruments of wood, bamboo, metal and bronze. Second, according to Khmer tradition, any of the vocal pieces may be transferred to an experience in instrumental performance. This might also mean that a song may be simultaneously sung and played, and that its melody may serve as an instrumental interlude between verses. Third, while the *roneat ek* characteristically plays melodies in octaves, this is probably not possible on Orff xylophones due to both their restricted range and also the lack of kinesthetic development of most young students for handling octaves. Still, students may be made aware of this performance technique through listening and discussion, which may lead to a fuller appreciation of the complexity of the music and its performance practice. Fourth, students should be encouraged to use two mallets in alternating fashion for playing successive pitches of a melody. Fifth, in the case of pitches of longer duration, a tremolo on the xylophone should be played with both mallets in order to sustain the sound through its designated time length. Working with young students will necessitate playing the most basic version. Older students will be more able to attempt the first steps at embellishments, tremolo, and playing in octaves.

Learning by Listening

While teachers may seek to develop in their students a repertoire of songs and instrumental experiences from Cambodia, the process by which Khmer music is transmitted should also be kept in mind. As music is transmitted orally by teacher to student in Cambodia, it is important that students here also be given the experience of learning by listening. If you intend to learn and/or teach this music with the goal being a performance, you are well advised to listen and re-listen to the tape—in the car, at meals, or while conducting routine tasks at home and in school. Immerse yourself and your students in the pronunciation and phrasing, style, timbre, accompaniment, rhythms and other subtleties that are impossible to record fully on paper. Gradually, the music and language will assume a level of familiarity and comfort in the ears of the previously uninitiated, and the vocal and instrumental pieces will be understood for their inherent beauty and logic. In the ideal situation, given the time and inclination for extended listening (and practice), music teachers will be able to present the music orally, to be received aurally by their students. In the classroom, students can also be presented with informal and unguided opportunities to listen (for example, while entering the room, during independent project time, in an art class as background for a related art project in shadow-puppetry, during a recess or free-play period) along with more formal presentations of the music.

River Scene. (Illustration by Tho Sangphet.)

I. Three Etiquette Songs for Small Children

In Cambodia, there are songs that describe planting and harvesting, songs that express joy and happiness, songs used in rituals at weddings and worship of the spirit ceremonies, and songs that carry political messages. There are songs sung principally by adults, and songs sung by children. Songs for children are often intended to teach them about nature, birds and animals, good manners and hygiene, and respect for elders. In 1972, my brother Yang Sam and I found ourselves in need of songs for teaching young children ages four to eight in Phnom Penh, so we selected traditional songs, and also composed some. They teach children when to say "thank you," to wake up on time for school, to watch traffic when crossing the road, to wash their hands before eating, to know and love birds and animals, and to appreciate the natural beauty of Cambodia, including trees and flowers.

Young children in Cambodia, as elsewhere in the world, learn about appropriate social behaviors through songs they sing. While good manners, respect for their elders, and proper hygiene can be taught through adult models, special attention is given to the importance of these and other behaviors within the culture when they are the subject of songs. Both educational and entertaining, the messages of these songs can be discussed so that children will be certain to put their ideas into practice. "Mun Pel Nhaim" was composed by Sam-Ang Sam and his brother; the next two songs are traditional. The recording features Sam-Ang Sam playing the *roneat ek and tror so* while his daughters Laksmi and Malene Sam sing.

Song 1: "Mun Pel Nhaim" [Before Mealtime]

Mun pel nhaim
makk phdaim oy leang dai
pruoh mean merok sen changrai
noam rumkhan.

Before meal time,
Mother tells me to wash my hands,
Because there are nasty germs,
Which can cause trouble.

Khnhomm rout reah
pranhapp minn akk khan
leang dai oy ban sa-at teup khnhomm
teou rork nhaim.

I hurry,
Not to forget,
To wash my hands clean, then I
Go to eat.

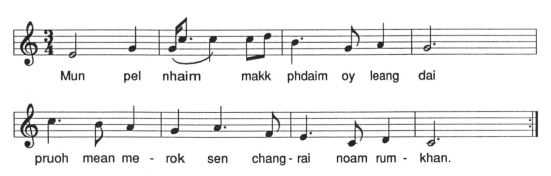

Song 2: "Doeur Roeu Keng" [Walk or Sleep]

Doeur roeu keng dang khluon oy trang
trauv damrang toan khluon neou kmeng
tuoh angkuy roeu muoy chhor leng
yeung kmeng kmeng chhor oy trang khluon.

While you walk or sleep, keep your body straight,
Straighten up while you are young,
Whether you play sitting or standing,
You are the young people who stand up straight.

Muk nhonhimm sangkhimm chea nich
komm be kich lorp meul kroy khnang

Smiling face with hope always,
Do not turn away hiding and looking from behind
the (someone's) back,

ngeup muk loeung niyeay chhloeuy chhlang
noeung neak phang teup hao klahan.

Raise your face and converse,
With others as a brave person.

Doeur roeu keng dang khluon oy trang trauv dam-rang toan khluon neou

kmeng tuoh ang-kuy roeu muoy chhor leng yeung kmeng kmeng chhor oy trang khluon.

Song 3: "Leang Dai" [Wash Hands]

Boeu dai yeung pralakk dey
komm chapp chamney roeu num aha
pruoh mean merok roeusya
kach chlaing kla praha yeung ban.

If our hands are dirty,
Do not touch desserts, cakes or foods,
There are nasty germs,
That are cruel and could kill us.

Dauchneh yeung trauv mni mnea
kamchatt pouch vea teup ban sokk san
leang dai noeung toeuk muoy chan
ruoch komm khan doh noeung sabou.

We must hurry,
To get rid of them for safety,
Wash your hands in a bowlful of water,
And do not forget to wash them with soap.

Boeu dai yeung pra lakk dey komm chapp cham ney roeu num a

mnea kam chatt pouch vea teup ban sokk

1

har pruoh mean me rok roeu sya kach khlaing kla pra ha yeung

san leang dai noeung toeuk muoy

2

ban. II. Dauch neh yeung trauv mni chan rouch komm khan doh noeung sa bou.

Study Guide:
Teaching/Learning Sequence   Level: early childhood, K and above

1. **Explore the sound and meaning of the Khmer language:**

➤ Pronounce the song texts, imitating the sounds heard on the tape. (Refer to the "Romanization of Khmer Words" guide.)

➤ Examine the meanings of the texts by referring to the translations.

➤ Practice speaking the following Khmer phrases gleaned primarily from the songs:

Leang dai	Say: *leé*-ing dah-ee	"Wash your hands"
Komm yum soka	Say: kohm yuhm saw-*káh*	"Don't cry"
Arkun	Say: aw-*koŏń*	"Thank you"
Nhonhimm	Say: nyoh-*nyihḿ*	"Smile"

➤ Learn other common Khmer phrases not found in these songs:

Chumreap suor	Say: choŏm-ree-up *soŏr*	"Hello"
Chumreap lea	Say: choŏm-ree-up *leé*-ah	"Goodbye"
Sokk sabbay te?	Say: sawk sahb-*báh*-ee tay?	"How are you?"
Sokk sabbay te.	Say: sawk sahb-*báh*-ee tay.	"I am fine."

➤ Note that the difference in Khmer between "How are you?" and "I am fine" is indicated by inflection alone: the first phrase uses the rising tone of questions, and the second the falling tone of statements. The word *khnhomm* precedes *sokk sabbay te* when addressing an older person, but is omitted when addressing someone of equal status. In addition, *lok* may be used as a sign of respect for a man, and *lok srey* for a woman.

➤ Practice the gesture that accompanies Khmer greetings and farewells. Place palms together with fingers pointing upward (as in prayer), hold them close to the chest, and bend slightly from just above the waist. While the chest level is suitable for greeting social equals, palms are raised to the chin for parents, elders, and authority figures, to the forehead for a king or monk, and above the head for addressing God. Practice changing from one level to the next.

2.   **For the Music Professional:** "Mun Pel Nhaim" [Before Mealtime] flows in a triple feeling, while both "Doeur Roeu Keng" [Walk or Sleep] and "Leang Dai" [Wash Hands] are in duple meter; listeners may find themselves swaying gently to the meter beat. The songs are centered in major tonality, and lay chiefly within the range of one octave.

➤ For each song, listen to the recording:
* Trace the rise and fall of the melody in the air
* Draw the melodic contour on the chalkboard or paper
* Conduct the meter beat (1 - 2   or   1- 2- 3)
                                   ↓ ↑   ↓ →↑

➤ For each song, prepare to sing:
* Pronounce each phrase in its melodic rhythm while conducting the pulse. Begin with "la" if necessary. Break phrases into sub-phrases if needed, and repeat without pause until the words begin to roll gently off the tongue.

➤ Sing each song:
* Sing "la" or the words while tapping the melodic rhythm.
* Treat each song phrase as if it were a solo/response form, as group follow in imitation the singing of the leader.
* Sing with and without the taped recording.

➤ Pick out the melody on any available instruments. Compare timbres.

Yang Sam

II. "Chapp Kaun Khleng": A Line-Game Song

Some games in Cambodia are played only by boys or only by girls, but "Chapp Kaun Khleng," [Catch the Baby Eagle], is traditionally played by all children throughout the country. Younger children learn the game from older children; it is not taught by teachers or other adults. We always played it especially during the Khmer New Year, which occurs during the month of April. The game is not only fun, but also teaches children to love and protect their families just like the hen cares for her baby chicks.

Traditional game songs are still sung by Khmer people of all ages, including children, adolescents and adults. In Cambodia and also in North American communities of Cambodians, the evening hours are frequently a favorite time for gathering to sing and play game songs.

In playing the "Chapp Kaun Khleng" [Catch the Baby Eagle] game, children gather together and assign one child, usually a taller, older, or stronger child, to act as the "hen" or leader of the group. Another child is designated as the "eagle," and the remaining children are the "chicks." The participants then look for small branches and twigs which they pile high for firewood and then ignite.

As the game proceeds, the hen orders all chickes to form a line, one behind the next. They hold tightly to the waist of the "chick" in front of them and begin to walk around the fire. The singing begins as the hen mocks the eagle: "Catch the baby eagle, play with the baby *ak* [a large bird]. The *popich* [a small bird] calls "my only baby." The hen continues:

> "Dig a hole, plant the *trakuon* [vine-like vegetable that grows
> in water]. As the rabbits hide, the *trakuon* grows well. A pair
> of candles, the umbrella shades the Buddha. Raise the hands
> and salute. Grandma asks for the fire."

The verse is a compilation of rhyming words, a set of unrelated phrases that describe everyday object and events in Cambodia.

In response to the hen's mock, the eagle approaches the hen and chicks and begins a dialogue with the hen:

Eagle: Grandma asks for the fire.
Hen: The fire is off. [There is no fire.]
Eagle: I ask for one chick.
Hen: Which one?
Eagle: The one in front.
Hen: No.
Eagle: The one in back.
Hen: Take it if you can catch it.

On hearing the reply, the eagle chases the last chick, and the other chicks as well. The chicks line up behind the hen for protection, grabbing the waist of the one in front of them. The snaking line of chicks moves back and forth behind the hen, who extends her arms to protect them from the eagle. Somewhat similar to tag and "Dungeon" in purpose, "Chapp Kaun Khleng" adds a distinctly Khmer flavor through the song which accompanies it. The game teaches alertness, caution and quick thinking and suggests to children the importance of protecting oneself and one's family.

Young people playing "Chapp Kaun Khleng" around a fire. (Illustration by Yang Sam.)

"Chapp Kaun Khleng" [Catch the Baby Eagle]

Verse 1:

Chapp kaun khleng   Catch the baby eagle,
praleng kaun ak   Play with the baby *ak*,
popich nhek nhak   The *popich* calls,
kaun anh te muoy.   "My only baby."

Verse 2:

Chik anlung   Dig a hole,
daim trakuon   Plant the *trakuon*,
tunsay rut puon   As the rabbits hide,
trakuon loeung loah.   The *trakuon* grows well.

Verse 3:

Tien muoy kou   A pair of candles,
taingyou baing preah   The umbrella shades the Buddha,
leuk dai sampeah   Raise the hands and salute,
daun daun somm phleung.   Grandma asks for the fire.

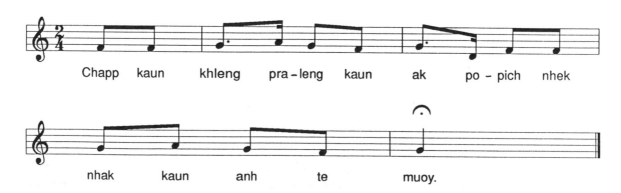

Study Guide
Teaching/Learning Sequence   Level: early childhood, K-2

1. Discuss the nature of a game song:

➤What other game songs do children know from their neighborhoods? From the schoolyards? From the classroom? ["Red Rover," "Ambos a Dos," "Bluebird," "Hokey Pokey," "Go In and Out the Window," jump rope chants like "Teddy Bear," hand game songs.]

* How is the song important to the game? Is the game the same minus the song?
* Do the words always make sense? Discuss the translation of this and other game songs.

2. Prepare to play the game:

➤First, sing along with the recording on the syllable "loo" while tapping the rhythm, then pronounce each phrase in rhythm. (Refer to the recording for correct pronunciation, since an accurate transcription of Khmer is impossible to write out simply.) As the group leader becomes more comfortable with the pronunciation, group members may follow each phrase in imitation, or use the recording as the leader, pausing the tape for the group to echo.

➤Play the game, (minus the fire, if necessary) encouraging children to sing as they play so that the game has "musical support." Sing the song in Khmer, and carry on the dialogue between the eagle and the hen in English if there are no Khmer speakers in the group.

3. For the Music Professional:
As is commonly found in children's songs, the melody of "Chapp Kaun Khleng" consists of four pitches within a comfortable vocal range of *d-a* (it is tetratonic). Note that the first phrase is similar to the second, and that the three verses provide ample opportunity to become acquainted with the tones of Khmer traditional children's songs.

➤Listen to the recording.
* How many phrases are there? [2]
Show the phrases by drawing curved lines in the air.
* Tap the pulse. Are all the rhythms smooth and even? (Choppy: ♩♪)
How many times does the choppy rhythm occur? (Twice.)

➤Sing the song on "loo" beginning with partial phrases, adding one pulse of the melody each time in a leader/response format. Retain a moderate tempo with no pauses or hesitation between phrases. Sing one verse at a time, leader/response format, or by listening to individual verses of the recording, then pausing the tape for the group to echo.

Khmer children playing "Leak Kensang." Illustration by Yang Sam.

A group of young adults playing "Chhoung." Illustration by Yang Sam.

III. "Leak Kanseng" and "Chhoung": Scarf Game Songs

I heard "Leak Kanseng" often when I was a young boy, and I played the game with my friends in the village of Bamnak where I lived. The origin of this popular song and game is unknown as it has never been recorded before, but it has been around for a long while. The "Leak Kanseng" game is usually played by children eight years and older, and sometimes by adolescents as well. Today, "Leak Kanseng" is seen and heard especially at the time of the special holidays such as New Year, the Soul of Ancestors Day in September, and the Flower Ceremony in October. As for the adult game "Chhoung," I did not have a chance to play it when I was a boy in Cambodia. I do, however, remember watching it played often in my village, and in the nearby temple compounds during the New Year celebrations. Now I sometimes play it with friends in Seattle, as do other adults in Cambodian communities throughout North America, and it is a favorite of Cambodian-American teenagers.

From an early age, Khmer children enjoy the song game called "Leak Kanseng" [Hiding the Scarf]. In an open space, children gather to sit in a circle and place their hands on their knees. One child holds the scarf as he or she walks on the outside of the circle, while all repeatedly sing the three-tone chant. After two or three trips around the circle, the "scarf-hiding" child places the scarf behind the back of one sitting child. If the "sitting" child is aware of the scarf placed behind him/her, s/he picks it up and chases the "scarf-hiding" child around the circle. The "scarf-hiding" child takes the space of the former sitting child, and the game begins anew as they change places and roles. (If the "sitting child" is not aware that the scarf has been left behind him, the "hider" runs around the circle, picks up the scarf, and taps it on the back of the "sitter.") The sitting child then rises, runs, and is chased around the circle and back to his original seat by the scarf-hider. This means that the game begins again with the same scarf-hider, who then chooses a new child behind which to drop the scarf.

"Leak Kanseng" [Hiding the Scarf]

Verse:

Leak kanseng!	Hide the scarf!
Chhma khaim keng!	The cat is biting his/her heel!
Oh long oh long.	And drags the leg.

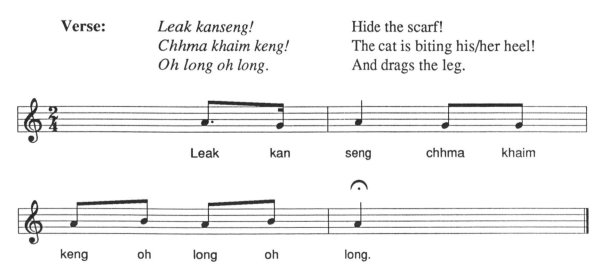

71

Another song game called "Chhoung" [The Scarf Ball] is played by Khmer adults during *chet* (April) or *pisak* (May), the months of the New Year celebrations. Two groups of men and women are formed facing each other at a distance of 25 or more feet. They take a scarf-ball (see below) and begin singing while tossing the *chhoung* "as high as the top of a coconut [or betel] tree." When men sing a verse, the women respond in vocables; when women begin, men sing the vocable response. After singing, a previously-designated leader shouts "chhoung euy chhoung" and throws the *chhoung* at the women who try to catch it. The woman who catches it throws it at the man of her choice, who becomes a prisoner of the women's side if he is hit. "Chhoung" is also played with a man trying to tag a woman, who then becomes a prisoner of the men's side. The game continues until all the men or all the women have been taken prisoners.

Both song games utilize a rectangular scarf resembling the traditional *krama* that is worn diagonally across the chest by women. (Men wear the *krama* wrapped around their hip when they work or bathe.) The *chhoung* is more than a scarf, however; it is a soft scarf-ball consisting of bundled material that forms the "head" and a long and free-flowing "tail" that trails as it flies through the air. The *chhoung* is easy to make, and affords a soft and harmless object as the focus of these song games.

"Chhoung" [The Scarf Ball]

Men:

Eu euy bang bah chhoung teou   I toss the *chhoung,*
thlai euy chhoung teu leu chong daung   It gets stuck at the top of the coconut
                                                                           tree,

kramomm chhor chraung thlai euy chaim   All the women stand;
    chapp chhoung bang.   Catch my *chhoung.*
Eu euy o na keo keo pi a o na na na   (Vocables.)
    keo euy.

Study Guide

Teaching/Learning Sequence   Level: early childhood; adult

1. Recall the traditional games that use cloth as "props" including "Blind Man's Bluff" (scarf blindfold), "Flag Tag" (flag or scarf), "Pin the Tail on the Donkey" (tack with scarf tail), the Vietnamese game "Xay Khan" [I am Shaking the Handkerchief], and the African-American game song "Little Johnny Brown." Discuss the significance of props in theater and in games, and consider the reasons behind their use in playing games and playing characters in stage productions. Also, consider for discussion the relationship between children's play, the games of children and adults, and theater.

2. Listen (numerous times) to the recording of "Leak Kanseng":
      * Provide a translation of the words.
      * Listen to the rhythm: what part sounds like the limping or dragging leg? [the phrase *leak kanseng*]

3. Listen (numerous times) to the recording of "Chhoung":
      * Provide a translation of the words.
      * Listen for the distinctive features of the singing style, including slides between pitches, trills and breaks as the melody leaps a wide interval.
      * Draw the shape of the melody in the air while listening.

4. Explore the poetry of "Chhoung":
"Chhoung" is set in an ancient formula for writing poetry that dates from the Funan-Chenla period (Funan was the first through sixth, Chenla was the sixth through ninth century A.D.). It has sixteen syllables that are characteristically divided into four sections of four syllables each.

➤Create a group or individual poem in this Khmer poetic formula.
      * Chant the new poem in a suitable rhythm.
      * Create a singable melody for the poem.

5. Compare these two traditional scarf-game songs.
      * Both utilize a scarf in the game.
      * Both have a similar rhythmic feel.
      * "Chhoung" utilizes vocables, sung syllables of no specific meaning, in addition to words of meaning.
      * "Leak Kanseng" is traditionally played by children, boys and girls in a mixed group, and is played in a circle; "Chhoung" is for adults and involves separate lines of men and women, facing each other.

6. Research and discuss the functional and symbolic role of scarves, handkerchiefs, belts and flags in a musical context.

➤Many societies employ scarves, handkerchiefs, belts, and flags. as a symbol of the interest or bond between a man and woman who are attracted to each other, are courting, are becoming engaged or are getting married. Others use them to keep a proper distance between dancers— they hold opposite ends of the cloth when it is not considered appropriate for them to touch hands. Sometimes a cloth is offered publicly during a dance as a gesture of betrothal, or at the least, as a sign of romantic linking. E.g.:

* A Chasidic Jewish bride and groom will be hoisted high in separate chairs by their dancing friends while the couple precariously grab opposite ends of a cloth napkin to stay near each other, but may not touch otherwise for a proscribed time.

* The African-American game song "Little Johnny Brown" is reminiscent of West African courting dances.

* There are many Peruvian and Ecuadorian dances for couples that involve shawls or scarves.

* Some Native American social dances require a cloth to maintain propriety between the male and female dancers (who rarely dance together in any case).

* Greek, Middle Eastern, and Eastern European dances frequently utilize a scarf or handkerchief, sometimes even when the dancers are all male or all female.

➤Find more examples, and photographs to illustrate, if possible.

Yang Sam

7. For the Music Professional: Like many children's chants, the melody of "Leak Kanseng" consists of three successive pitches set within the narrow range of a major third. "Chhoung" represents the more expansive range of adult songs, encompassing an octave and a third. Both songs are felt in duple meter, although "Chhoung" moves in compound four-pulse units that utilize sophisticated rhythms and extremely ornamented melodies.

➢Listen to "Leak Kanseng":
   * How many phrases are there? [1]
   * Listen for and conduct the downbeats: How many measures are there?[3]
   * How many pitches are there? [3] Sing them.
   * Listen to the rhythm: what part sounds like a dragging leg? [the anacrusis and downbeat on the text "leak kanseng": ♩. ♪ ♩
   leak kanseng
   * Chant "leak kanseng" while limping to its rhythms: ♩. ♪ ♩ ♩. ♪ ♩
   leak kan-seng leak kan- seng

➢Listen to "Chhoung":
   * Listen for separate syllables, phonemes, and vocal sounds. Note features of the singing style.
   * Listen for high and low pitches, for ascending and descending contours of the melody—the rising and falling shape.
   * Listen and hum along with the melody. Is the range of pitches wide or narrow? [wide] Show the expansive range by drawing it in space while listening.
   * Listen while following the notation. Do the transcribed notes include all the sounds you are hearing? [No. These notes are just the basic framework for the many embellishments which are included as part of the melody.]
   * Listen to determine the pulse and meter of "Chhoung." [4/4] Conduct the pulse.
   * How many phrases are there? How many times does the singer take a breath? [4 two-measure phrases]

➢Compare the two songs:
   * Both are felt in duple meter.
   * "Leak Kanseng" is a chant using a narrow vocal range; the melody of "Chhoung" is wide in range.
   * "Leak Kanseng" has only one three-measure phrase; the eight measures in "Chhoung" can be divided into music of two phrases (or four sub-phrases).

➢Sing each song:
   * Hum the melody while tapping its rhythm.
   * Slowly chant the words in rhythm. Repeat as necessary.
   * Phrase by phrase, slowly sing the words.
   * Introduce the games, continuing to sing. Encourage participants to sing while playing, reminding the group that the sung accompaniment is critical to the success of the game.

IV. "Sarika Keo": Song of the Colorful Bird

The song "Sarika Keo" is very popular in Cambodia and in North America because it portrays an important part of Khmer life. As it refers to the sarika keo bird, it personifies nature in all of its beauty and color. My friends and I learned it from the primary school teacher in our village when we were little, and I never forgot it. I have since taught "Sarika Keo" to my children, who enjoy singing it with their friends.

In Cambodia, birds of many colors reside in wooded areas and in tall grasses of the Mekong River Delta. They include the *sek, moan prey, totea, krasa, kruoch, lolork, kokk, tung,* and *popich*. Some birds have been domesticated and are kept by people as pets. The *sarika keo* is a small black bird with white and yellow markings on the sides of its head. It is among the most beautiful of birds, and the Khmer enjoy training it to speak words and phrases such as "A vorng euy" (a phrase used to call a bird), "Teou na?" [where are you going] and "Arkun" [thank you]. The *sarika keo* is the subject of one of the most popular songs in all of Cambodia. Children learn the song while learning also about the bird, how it eats, plays, sings and dances.

The song may be sung by girls or women, with male singers contributing the vocables "Ey sariyaing" at the close of the first two phrases. The reverse is also true, such that when boys or men sing the verse, the girls and women sing only the vocables. All sing twice the response "Euy keo keo euy" as a conclusion to each verse. These are meant to sound like the call of the *sarika keo* bird.

The *sarika keo*. (Illustration by Tho Sangphet.)

"Sarika Keo"

Verse 1:

Sarika keo euy		Girls:	Oh! Sarika keo,
si ey kang kang?			What are you eating?
Ey sariyaing. (2x)		Boys:	[Vocables]

Si phle dambang		Girls:	You are eating cactus fruits,
prachoeuk knea leng.			You are playfully nipping at each other.
Euy keo keo euy. (2x)		Boys:	[Vocables]

Verse 2:

Slap vea chakk kbach		Boys:	With your wing you dance,
moat vea thveu phleng.			With your beak you sing.
Ey sariyaing. (2x)		Girls:	[Vocables]

Prachoeuk knea leng		Boys:	You nip at each other,
leu mek proeuksa.			On the tree branch.
Euy keo keo euy. (2x)		Girls:	[Vocables]

77

Study Guide
Teaching/Learning Sequence   Level: grade 2 - adult

1. Introduce the song through a discussion of birds, their appearance and habitats. Show photographs of birds from various regions including birds that reside in the mountains, near the sea, in marshlands, along rivers. Show photos of soaring falcons and eagles, the technicolor feathers of South American birds used in clothing, black crows, pet parakeets. Try to recall other songs that imitate birds or feature them in the words or game, including the Hebrew "Kukuriku," "The Cuckoo" songs from Appalachia, "Viri Noka" [Messenger Bird] from the Chacos region of Argentina, and "Little Bird, Little Bird, Fly Through My Window" from South Carolina.

2. Listen to the recording of "Sarika Keo":
> * Provide a translation of the words.
> * Sing the melody softly on "loo" while listening to the words.
> * Join in on the vocables, "ey sariyaing," which functions as a response to the verse.

3. For the Music Professional: "Sarika Keo" is an example of a binary AB song, featuring sub-phrases of variable length: 8, 8, 6, and 10 pulses. The pentatonic melody begins with a long anacrusis, which begins the second similar phrase as well. This is a song that may be performed vocally or with an instrumental ensemble including recorders accompanied by xylophone ostinati, *chhing* and drum. The xylophone parts are not difficult to master, and provide a very traditional sound quality to accompany the singing.

> ➤Listen again to "Sarika Keo"
> * How many phrases are there? [4]
> * Do any phrases sound similar? [Phrase 1 and phrase 2]
> * Conduct the meter of the song. What is the meter of the song? [Duple]

> ➤Prepare to sing the song:
> * Note features of the singing style.
> * Play and sing the pitches of this pentatonic scale.

> * Sing the following pitch patterns in preparation for learning the song. (The group is in imitation of the teacher.)

➤Sing the song:
   * Sing the melody softly on a neutral syllable while listening to the words.
   * Sing the vocables, listening carefully to the other parts.
   * Sing each phrase in imitation of the singer on the tape.
   * Divide the singers into two groups: (1) verse singers and (2) vocables.
   Both groups sing the last line of each verse, "euy keo keo euy." Reverse
   roles.
   * When the song is learned, add the *chhing* and drum parts, doubling voices
   with the recorders. Add the xylophone parts.

➤Prepare a performance featuring an ensemble using voices, recorders, finger cymbals,
drum and xylophone ostinati as written in the full transcription.

V. "Bakkha": Khmer Action Song

"Bakkha" (or "baksa") is the Khmer word for bird. It is also an action song that requires the performance of bird-like movements. I learned it from my teacher at the University of Fine Arts when I was about sixteen or seventeen years old. My children learned this song at home when they were still quite young. As they sing it, they also perform the gestures of the dance that accompanies it.

Cambodian dancers traditionally begin their study at a very young age, when the body is flexible and can be trained to move in ways that might be impossible if attempted later in life with no prior preparation. A new generation of Cambodian-Americans is beginning to make the commitment to court dance training, taking great pride in their progress. Some of the teenagers have the proper attitude and stance, and yet will never master the intricate hand, arm and foot gestures completely because the period of genocide, war and flight out of Cambodia prohibited them from training at the most advantageous age. Yet when they perform, these dedicated teenagers exhibit grace and glow with pride over the wonderful progress they have made.

There is a small repertoire of songs in Khmer tradition that are classified as "action songs," or songs that require stylized gestures of the dance to accompany it. "Bakkha" is one of the first songs learned by children seeking training in the court music and dancer of Cambodia. Not only is "Bakkha" considered a specific dance work, but the melody is apt to be played by a *pinn peat* or *mohori* ensemble during the opening exercises of a dance rehearsal.

The *Sek Sarika* [parrot dance] showing Laksmi Sam using
stylized bird gestures. (Photo by Sam-Ang Sam.)

"Bakkha"

Verse 1:   *Preah peay phay phatt*   The wind blows the flowers
                  bopha phall (2x)
               Pidor dett dall duong   The fragrance touches my heart.
                  haroeutey.

Verse 2:   *Neary neang chrieng roam*   Girls sing and dance and play to be famous
                  leng oy lbey (2x)
               Pothisatt phlomm pey totuol   Bodhisatva plays the pipe in the music.
                  phleng.

Verse 3:   *Ang intri dauch neary*   The goddess is like a lady in the
                  srey suor than (2x)   heavenly world
               Srey suor thett dett vimean   The heavenly lady resides in heaven.
                  than yeamea.

Chan Moly Sam coaching her dance students, (l. to r.), Malene Sam, Laksmi Sam and Rithmaly Hay. She is helping the youngest stretch more. Notice the position of their left leg. (Photo Bonnie Periale.)

Malene Sam doing a warming-up exercise. (Photo Bonnie Periale.)

"Bakkha"

Study Guide

Teaching/Learning Sequence   Level: grade 4 - adult

1. Read the translation of the text, and discuss the importance of music and dance in the lives of the people in traditional Cambodia. The words to the song mention Bodhisatva who may be described as "the enlightened one," a manifestation of the Buddha. "Goddess" refers to one of the many heavenly dancers of the royal courts of Cambodia.

> ➤Examine photographs of dancers:
>   * Examine the photographs that feature court (classical) dancers in graceful poses and adorned in magnificent gold-gilded costumes and headdresses. (See Chapter 3.)
>   * View the photographs of children of different ages learning and demonstrating various dance postures. Try to imitate the postures. This will probably hurt!
>   * Keeping in mind the translation, create gestures to communicate the meaning of the text of "Bakkha."
>   * Body language varies from culture to culture. Find some examples of common meanings expressed through body language in your family/community.

2. Listen to the recording:
    * Move rhythmically to the music.
    * Note features of the singing style, including the many pitches for a single syllable.
    * Hum, or sing the melody softly on "loo" while listening to the words.

3. For the Music Professional: The melody of "Bakkha" is an active one, in which the singer must catch a breath at the end of a florid phrase when, at last, there is a sustained pitch and resting point. The melody is set in a major tonality, but the listener may be surprised to hear a lowered seventh degree in all cases in which the leading tone might otherwise be expected.

> ➤Listen to the recording:
>   * Conduct the meter of the song in [a] slow two and [b] fast four.
>   * How many resting points of longer duration are there in the melody?[3]
>   * Map the rise and fall of the melody.

> ➤Sing the song:
>   * Sing the melody measure by measure or in short phrases, first with and then without the tape as accompaniment, using the Khmer words.
>   * Tackle longer phrases with each repetition.

➤Prepare a performance featuring an ensemble using voices, recorders, finger cymbals, drum and xylophone ostinati as written in the full transcription.

VI. "Thung Le": A Beginners' Instrumental Piece

Like many other Khmer melodies, the origin and meaning of "Thung Le" is unknown. I learned this piece when I was a young student at the University of Fine Arts in Phnom Penh. It can be played on nearly any of the traditional instruments including flute, fiddle, zither, dulcimer, xylophone or shawm. The melody is played in concerts, as accompaniment to dance performances, and is suitable as a "teaching piece," partly because it is one of the shortest pieces known, and it has such a simple melody. Even today, I teach it to my students on various instruments.

"Thung Le" is an example of entertainment music. It is among the first pieces learned by beginning instrumental students. It is presented here on both the *khloy* [flute] and *roneat* [xylophone]. The *khloy* is very similar to a recorder.

A typical scene in the countryside: a young cattle herder takes a break under a huge tree to play the *khloy* while a water buffalo walks by. (Illustration by Tho Sangphet.)

Study Guide
Teaching/Learning Sequence   Level: grade 4 - adult

1. Disuss the importance of instrumental music in the Khmer royal courts. (See Chapter 3 and Lesson 7.) Look at the photographs of the major Khmer instruments, including those heard performing this piece, the *khloy* and the *roneat*. The *khloy* is very similar to the recorder. List the similarities. The *roneat* is very similar to classroom xylophones. Note these similarities as well.

2. Listen to the recording:
> * Note that the melody is played twice: plainly, as notated here, and then in a more ornamented version.
> * Listen to both the *khloy* (version 1) and the *roneat* (version 2).
> * Hum the melody while listening to the recording.

3. For the Music Professional: An anacrusis opens each of two phrases, which feature alternating quarter- and eighth-notes and occasionally longer durations. The melody explores higher pitches first, and then drops an octave lower before returning to the song's starting pitch. Of special interest is the way in which the last pitch in each phrase is preceded by the same four-beat melodic phrase (measure 4 and 8), serving as a formulaic cadential figure.

> ➤Listen to the recording:
> > * Tap the pulse of the music: clap once every four beats; clap on beat 1: conduct beats 2, 3, and 4.
> > * Step the beat of the music while conducting.
> > * Step in a direction of choice for the first phrase, changing directions for the second phrase.

> ➤Hum the melody:
> > * While listening to the recording and then without the recording.
> > * While tapping the pulse; while stepping the pulse and changing directions per phrase.

> ➤Play the melody on recorder:
> > * Review fingerings for the recorder.
> > * Leader plays then group plays small melodic units or phrases in imitation.
> > * Combine phrases. Bring to tempo of recording.
> > * Sing letter names of notated piece while fingering the recorder.

➤Play the melody on xylophone: note the use of tremelos on longer pitches
   * Gesture the tremolo technique (of rapid alternation of mallets on one key) each time the tremolo is heard on longer pitches.
   * Begin with small melodic units to imitate; play separate phrases; combine them.
   * Sing letter names of notated piece while softly touching the keys with the index fingers.
   * Play at tempo.
   * Alternate between playing and humming.

➤Designate someone to play the *chhing*. Sound the muffled "chhepp" on the first pulse of each measure in alternation with the more ringing sound of "chhing" on the third pulse. See notation of "Thung Le" for guidance.

➤Discuss musical themes, ornamentation and embellishment by selecting specific pieces from a variety of musical styles—e.g., Baroque, rock, Broadway show tunes, jazz—and encourage group members to bring in recorded examples to illustrate.

"Thung Le"

VII. A Sampler of Instrumental Sounds

At sixteen while a student at the University, I began to learn the two-stringed fiddle called tror chhe [high-pitched fiddle] from my teacher, Master Yim Sem. I had already had a year or so of violin, and so found the tror chhe an appropriate next step. Later on, I also studied and eventually specialized on various wind instruments including khloy, pey pork, pey praboh, and sralai. Sralai was the most difficult because of the control one needs to play it. It is possible to get three pitches for the same fingering, depending on your breath and position of the tongue. My teachers also included Master Sek Ouch, Master Long Samreth, Master Thoeung, and Master Chhuon. Khmer wind instruments are still the most favorite for me to play. These instruments are taught in Cambodia even today, both at the University of Fine Arts and in the villages. Perhaps because of the great difficulty in mastering wind instruments, especially the technique of circular breathing, they are seldom selected by students for study.

The music of Cambodia includes a rich variety of wind, string, and percussion instruments. While ensembles commonly represent the court music of the Khmer courts, there are solo repertoires for many of the instruments—inside the courts and outside as well. (See Chapter 3 for photos and discussion of instruments and ensembles.) Some Khmer instruments resemble those found in China, India, or other parts of Southeast Asia, which attest to cross-cultural influences over the centuries. Certain characteristic features of Khmer music, however, are indicative that an instrument from another tradition was adapted and taken into the hearts of Khmer musicians and their listeners.

Instrument designs and musical ideas flow with the movement of humans across the artificial boundaries that are the borders of countries. On the surface, a listener might find similarities between Khmer, Thai, and Laotian music. This is no wonder, as these Southeast Asian peoples have shared aspects of language, literature, religion, and dance as well as music and musical instruments. Some scholars suggest that there may have been extensive borrowing among these cultures, and yet there are distinctions as well. For example, Thai music is played faster than Khmer music, and Khmer music tends to use more sustained or dotted rhythms and fewer running passages than the Thai. Cambodia's neighbors—Thailand, Laos, China, Vietnam and Indonesia—include instruments that are very similar to those found in Cambodia. The *khloy*, *sralai*, *tror so*, *khimm*, *roneat*, *korng vung* and *chhing* are similar to instruments found in Thailand and Laos. The *tror so* and *khimm* are similar to instruments found in China, and the *roneat* is similar to xylophones found in Burma and Indonesia.

In general, the most prevalent instruments in a culture give indications of the relative abundance of certain natural resources in the country. Gongs, bells, metal buzzers, lamellae (and metal drum bodies indicate metal ores and smelting operations (such as would be found in parts of Africa). The presence of a large variety of wooden drums requires trees of the appropriate diameter and hardness of wood. Gourd rattles are found where the climate allows a long, relatively dry growing season. Flutes call for hollow reeds or woods that can be hollowed out without breaking or splitting. Complex instruments that are also elaborately fashioned and decorated in some cases reflects a relatively sedentary society as opposed to a nomadic one. It is easy to see the reflection of the climate and natural resources in the materials used to create the principal instruments of Cambodia. The most common materials used are bamboo, hard woods, rattan, copper and bronze.

The major categories referred to in the "Sachs-Hornbostel classification system": aerophones (winds), chordophones (strings), membranophones (drums) and idiophones (xylophones, gongs, and instruments that can be shaken, scraped or stamped) are well-represented among the traditional Khmer instruments you will hear on the companion recording. (For more detailed descriptions and discussion of Khmer instruments, see Chapter 3.)

Some Relatives of Khmer Instruments

Khmer Name:	Thai/Lao Name:	Chinese:	Burmese:	Indonesian:
khloy	khlui			
sralai	pi		huè	
tror so	saw duang	erhu		
khimm	kim	yang chin		
roneat	ranat		pattala	gambang
korng vung	khong wong		kyi-waing	
chhing	ching			

A Sampler of Instrumental Sounds As Presented on Tape:

#: Name:	Description:	Title:
1. khloy	bamboo duct or fipple flute	"Khmer Changkeh Reav" [Slim-waisted Khmer]
2. pey pork	single free-reed bamboo pipe	"Surin" [Lost Province of Cambodia]
3. sralai	quadruple-reed shawm	"Chhouy Chhay" [Khmer Princess]
4. tror so	two-stringed fiddle	"Khyall Chumno Khe Praing" [Gentle Breeze of the Dry Season]
5. khimm	hammered dulcimer	"Loeung Preah Punlea" [Getting on the Pavilion]
6. roneat ek	wooden or bamboo xylophone, high-pitched	"Khmer Krang Phka" [Khmer String Flowers]
7. roneat thung	wooden or bamboo xylophone, low-pitched	"Chenn Choh Touk" [Chinese Get on the Boat]
8. korng vung	circular frame gongs	"Sinuon" [a cool color; mix of white and yellow]
9. chhing	small cymbals	rhythm patterns

Study Guide
Teaching/Learning Sequence   Level: grade 4 - adult

1. Precede listening experiences by discussing interesting issues that will provide a general foundation for understanding instruments and instrumental music of Cambodia. Explore ideas such as these:

➤What sorts of materials are instruments made of?(woods, metals, plastics, reeds)

* Considering the climate and topography, what sorts of materials would you expect Cambodians to use in constructing their musical instruments?(bamboo, hard woods, rattan, copper, bronze)

~Discuss instruments of other countries in terms of their materials.

~Discuss instruments made of "found objects" such as the steel drums of Trinidad.

~Discuss instruments found in the United States, grouping them by construction material, ethnic origin, development, and current usage (e.g., The banjo, originally made of gourd, skin, gut and wood is now commonly made of metal, plastic, steel strings and metal reinforced ebony neck with metal tuning pegs; arrived with enslaved Africans, was used in minstrel shows, Broadway, and then was picked up by Bluegrass, "country" and folk musicians.)

➤Would you expect any of Cambodia's neighbors to share some of the same instruments? Refer to a map of Asia, and note that some of Cambodia's instruments are similar in shape and sound to those found in Thailand and Laos, China and Indonesia.

* Explore the idea that music can cross artificial political borders, and research examples of this happening, similar to the way in which Mexican traditional music is commonly heard in southern California, Arizona, New Mexico and much of Texas. (Other examples might include "Pan-Indian" musical styles that have evolved on the Native American pow-wow circuit.)

➤Would you expect Cambodia's musical instruments to represent the major categories of instruments in the "Sachs-Hornbostel Classification System"? Refer to this system, detailed on the previous page and Chapter 3) in order to determine HOW the sounds are produced.

* Similarly, are there any countries or cultures you can think of that might not have the natural resources to provide materials for construction of instruments that would fall within each of the categories?

2. Listen to the recordings.

➤Consider: (a) the material the instrument is constructed from; (b) other cultures that might share a similar instrument; and (c) the manner in which the instrument produces sound, which determines the category of the instrument in the Sachs-Hornbostel Classification System.

3. For the music professional: In several additional listenings, group members may be led to describe the melodic and rhythmic features of the featured pieces and passages. The greater the exposure to the music, the more likely it is they will grow in understanding of and appreciation for it.

➢Point out the tremendous skill necessary to perform on the traditional instruments of Cambodia.

* Note the difficult technique of circular breathing used in the performance of wind instruments such as *khloy, pey pork,* and *sralai* (see explanation, page-).
* Observe the way in which the *tror so* melody tends to include sliding between main pitches, a musical feature that can be readily performed on various fiddles and lutes.
* Observe also the tremolo technique for sustaining pitches of longer duration on the *roneat.*

➢The music of Cambodia sometimes functions to tell stories or set scenes. In many instances, only one particular piece is appropriately used to accompany a certain event, function, or situation. For example, Lesson 12: Boxing Music concentrates on the piece that is the traditional accompaniment for boxing matches because of its unique characteristic of effectively stimulating boxers to be in the right mood and pace to fight. Similarly, the pieces called "Cheut Chapp" and "Saloma" have always been used to accompany combat scenes during the large shadow play, masked play and court dance performances. The Khmer are culturally bound to match piece and mood.

* Discuss the association of each piece's title with the mood or images that are presented by the performing instrument.
* Find programmatic pieces from other traditions, such as Smetana's "The Moldau," or Dukas' "The Sorcerer's Apprentice," or Saint Saen's "Carnival of the Animals" to compare. Write or draw impressions of any of these works, or others that convey drama through music.

VIII. "Khmer Changkeh Reav": [Slim-Waisted Khmer]

In Cambodia, children usually choose and learn their instruments as they like. The roneat is among the most favorite instruments to learn, even among young Cambodian students in North America. Beginning students often work with mallets that have been tied together with a piece of string that is just the length of the octave. Once their muscles learn and remember the proper distance for the octave interval automatically, the string is cut or untied. As the roneat is the lead instrument in several traditional ensembles, the roneat performer is under greater pressure to perform well. I myself have learned the roneat casually, and practice it when I have the time.

The xylophone known as *roneat* is an important melody instrument in Khmer instrumental ensembles, including the *pinn peat* and the *mohori* of the court traditions. The origin of the *roneat* is obscure, although there are similar xylophones found in Thailand, Laos, Burma, Malaysia, and Indonesia. There are several sizes of both wooden, bamboo and metal *roneat*, including *roneat ek* (a 21-key high-pitched xylophone), *roneat thung* (a 16-key low-pitched xylophone), *roneat dek* (21-key high-pitched metallophone), and *roneat thong* (16-key low-pitched metallophone). Padded mallets are used to play the *roneat* in ensembles to accompany the court dance, masked plays, shadow plays, and for religious ceremonies. (See photos in Chapter 3 and Lesson IX.)

"Khmer Changkeh Reav" [Slim-Waisted Khmer] is a singing piece played by the *mohori* ensemble for entertainment. The instruments used on the companion tape are the *roneat ek*, *korng tauch* (high-pitched circular frame gongs) and *korng thomm* (low-pitched circular frame gongs). They are playing simultaneous melodic variations of one principal melody.

A *pinn peat* ensemble, showing two players performing on the *korng tauch* and *korng thomm* circular frame gongs. To the left in the photo is Sam-Ang Sam playing *sralai*, *roneat* players in front, and the large, deep sounding barrel drums *skor thomm*, rear center. (Photo by Frank Proschan.)

"Khmer Changkeh Reav"

Roneat Ek

Korng
Tauch

Korng
Thomm

Study Guide
Teaching/Learning Sequence   Level: Grade 4 through Adult

1. **Show the photographs of the Khmer *roneat* that appear below and in Chapter 3 and Lesson IX.** Note the sloping shape of the resonance box of the *roneat*, and the padded mallets.

   ➤Compare the size and shape of the instruments with other types of xylophones and metallophones including marimbas, vibraphones, Indonesian *gambang*, and West African *balafon* as well as with the barred instruments of the Orff Schulwerk instrumentarium.

2. **Listen to the recording of "Khmer Changkeh Reav":**
   * The first section is by the entire ensemble.
   * Each instrument then plays solo: first the *roneat ek* plays the basic and then an elaborated melody, then the *korng tauch* and finally the *korng thomm* play individually before a final run-through as an ensemble.

3. **For the music professional:** Using the melodic barred instruments of Africa and Southeast Asia as models (including those found in Java, Thailand, and Cambodia), the German composer and pedagogue Carl Orff collaborated with instrument-maker Karl Maendler to develop instruments suitable for performance by children. While the "Orff xylophones" do not retain the Southeast Asian cradle-shaped resonance boxes over which the bars are strung, their instrumental timbre bears a strong resemblance to the *roneat*. When young performers are presented with occasions for the performance of traditional instrumental music, their active involvement often increases their intrigue and propels them to further study. Thus, the xylophones and metallophones of the Orff instrumentarium may be a key to understanding the Khmer *roneat*, its melodic possibilities, and the heterophonic texture resulting from the simultaneous performance of several *roneat* in a *pinn peat* ensemble.

   ➤Listen to the tape for the <u>basic</u> melody on *roneat ek*:
   * There are two melodic pitches per measure, beginning with the first complete measure. Use numbers or solfege syllables to sing them.
   * On "loo," sing the melody played by the *roneat*.
   * Clap on beat 1; tap the back of the right hand on the palm of the left hand on beat 3.
   * Add the *chhing* pattern on finger cymbals beginning with measure 3.

   ➤Listen to the tape for the <u>elaborated</u> melody of the *roneat ek*:
   * Follow the principal melodic pitches.
   * Follow the notated melody of the *roneat*.
   * Sing the numbers or solfege syllables of the principal melodic pitches while the *roneat* plays a more complex melody.

* Sing the melody of the *roneat*.
* Clap on beat 1; tap the back of the right hand on the palm of the left hand on beat 3.

➤In small segments, play the melody of the *roneat ek*:
* Sing phrase one. Repeat.
* Sing while patting melodic rhythm on lap.
* Play on xylophone or metallophone.
* Learn additional phrases in a similar way, by first singing, then patting, and then playing the melody.

➤Listen to the tape for the melody of the *korng tauch* (which can be played on a xylophone or metallophone).
* Follow sequence above.
* Combine the two melodies of the *roneat* and *korng tauch*.

➤Listen to the tape for the melody of the *korng thomm* (which can be played on a xylophone or metallophone).
* Follow sequence above.
* Combine all three melodies.

➤Add the *chhing* as the timekeeper of the ensemble, similar to Lesson 6: "Thung Le."

Sam-Ang Sam playing *roneat ek*. The man with back turned to us is playing *khimm*. (Photo by Winnie Lambrecht.)

95

IX. "Khvann Tung": The *Mohori* Ensemble

I must have first heard the mohori when I was a young boy, but I didn't pay much attention to it at the time. Often, we heard the mohori in the neighbor's homes when, after dinner, musicians would get together and play just for fun. When I entered the University I began to hear it regularly, was attracted to it, and began to play in the ensemble myself. It was then that I realized the serious and more formal functions of the ensemble. The piece we recorded for the companion tape is very old—really a historical piece. The title has been passed on as "Khvann Tung" to each generation of students with no further translation. It is so old, and the literal meaning so obscure that no musician knows the exact translation. Each individual word cannot be translated precisely any more, so what we have included here is the general meaning.

Mohori is the name of a bird, and refers to both the musical ensemble and its repertoire. It has three main functions: it is the principal Khmer entertainment ensemble at banquets and other functions; it accompanies folk dances; and accompanies performances of the *mohori* theater. The ensemble is comprised of percussion, wind, and string instruments, including *roneat ek* and *roneat thung* (high-pitched and low-pitched xylophones), *khloy* (flute), *tror chhe* (high-pitched two-stringed fiddle), *tror so tauch* (medium-high-pitched two-stringed fiddle), *tror so thomm* (medium-low-pitched two-stringed fiddle), *tror ou* (low-pitched two-stringed fiddle), *krapeu* (zither), *khimm* (hammered dulcimer), *chhing* (small cymbals), and *thaun-rumanea* (drum-pair). There are no brass or reed instruments of any sort in the *mohori* ensembles. Its size is dependent upon patronage and ownership. The *mohori* ensemble performs songs that alternate between vocalist and the full ensemble, with the vocalist singing one or two verses followed by the instrumental performance of one or two cycles of music. The *mohori* theater includes singing, dancing and acting, presented in many ways like works for opera. The music and songs are drawn only from the *mohori* repertoire and accompanied only by the *mohori* ensemble. (Each type of theater is distinctive, using music and themes drawn from the specific repertoire of the ensemble that accompanies it.) It is a contemporary theater genre, developed over the past two decades or so primarily by the teachers and students of the University of Fine Arts in Phnom Penh. The costumes are not elaborate like those of the court performances, but due to the nature of the ensemble tend to be folk dress, very light, simple, and impressionistic. One popular theme deals with the remorse of a hunter, who went to the forest and killed a couple of birds who happened to be husband and wife. He was upset in the end by what he had done. Costumes for this piece include bird wings made of flowing lengths of cloth tied to the wrists to simulate flying movments as the arms are moved during the dances. The hunter has a bow, but nothing more elaborate. This piece has been performed in America many times, particularly during the New Year celebration, in Seattle, and in Washington D.C.

"Khvann Tung," the traditional piece performed on the companion tape, is a love poem that describes the beauty of a young woman and her captivating, bright voice. The words generally say that everyone wants to listen to her to understand the meaning of the words she sings.

A *mohori* ensemble. Performers include left to right: To Hear, *tror so*; Sam-Ang Sam, *khloy*; Bun Soth, *skor arakk*; Khandarith Hay, *chhing*. Hidden behind is a *sampho* player. (Photo by Bonnie Periale.)

The *roneat ek* (high-pitched xylophone) is commonly part of a *mohori* ensemble. (Photo by Sam-Ang Sam.)

"Khvann Tung" (First Cycle of Instrumental Version)

Study Guide
Teaching/Learning Sequence   Level: Grade 4 through Adult

1. Show photograph of the _mohori_ ensemble. Identify the string, wind, and percussion instruments, and comment on their similarities to familiar orchestral, popular and folk instruments.

➤Compare this type of musical drama with the Japanese Kabuki or Noh tradition, the Chinese Peking Opera, and the gamelan tradition of Indonesia that accompanies particular dance and theater pieces.

2. For the Music Professional: Refer to the following page of scales and pitches.

➤Sing on a neutral syllable the principal melodic pitches of "Khvann Tung."
   * Present them in small segments (for example, measures 1-5, 6-10, 11-16), to be sung repeatedly until the melodic contours and specific pitches have become familiar to the group.
   * While conducting in 4/4 meter, sing the combined smaller segments as a complete song.

➤Sing the C-Major scale in a slow and steady tempo, then the C pentatonic, leaving out the fourth and seventh degrees. Add the fourth and flatted seventh degrees to the scale. Finally, sing the scale-like melody that reinforces the unusual but critical fourth (and sometimes flatted) seventh degrees of "Khvann Tung."

➤Learn the _chhing_ (or finger cymbals) part. Allow the cymbals to ring brightly on the "o" symbols while saying "chhing," and to produce a muffling effect on the "+" symbols while saying "chhepp." Add the _chhing_ sounds while singing the principal melodic pitches.

➤As students sing and sustain the principal pitches, play the decorative "in-between" pitches on xylophone or on piano.

➤Listen to the first verse of "Khvann Tung."
   * As the singer performs the melody, follow the "chhing" and "chhepp" sounds. Play the _chhing_ with the recording.
   * Conduct the 4/4 meter while singing the principal melodic pitches in the key of the recording. Note the ornamental quality of the melody between the principal pitches.

➤Attempt to sing or play a small portion of the ornamented melody.

➤Listen to the complete piece. While conducting or playing the _chhing_, follow its typical Khmer form of vocal, instrumental, vocal, and instrumental sections.

"Khvann Tung"

Scales (In B-flat on the tape.)

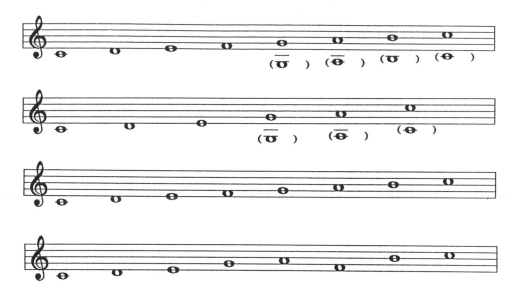

Principal Pitches (In B-flat on the tape.)

X. "Loeung Preah Punlea" [Getting on the Pavilion]: A Musical Story

"Loeung Preah Punlea" is one of my favorite pieces. It is among the most popular of Khmer pieces to play in mohori and pinn peat ensembles. It reminds me and all Khmer of the well-known story of Rithisen and Neang Kangrey, which we have only summarized here, because it is a long story with many versions.

"Loeung Preah Punlea" [Getting on the Pavilion] is a small work for *mohori* whose lyric is extracted from the story of Neang Kangrey, who expresses her sadness at losing her beloved Prince Rithisen. She wonders what she has done to cause her prince to leave her.

The Giantess Santhamea, Prince Rithisen and the Bag of Eyes. (Illustration by Tho Sangphet.)

The Story of Prince Rithisen and Neang Kangrey

Once upon a time, there was a widowed giantess named Santhamea who lived in a palace with her daughter, Neang Kangrey. Because she was always very hungry Santhamea had villagers from the area brought to her every day as her food. In the village lived a poor couple with twelve daughters, all very beautiful. One day Santhamea saw the twelve daughters, and because they were more beautiful than her daughter, she plucked their eyes out and stored them in a glass in a secret room in her palace.

The daughters grew up, and the youngest had a baby named Rithisen. He grew to be a handsome young man who took good care of his mother and eleven aunts, who lived with him deep in a cave. Meanwhile, Santhamea's unceasing jealousy and hatred of this family continued to be expressed in deviant ways. She decided to play a trick that would result in the death of Rithisen. Santhamea sent a messenger to demand that Rithisen carry a message to her own daughter, Neang Kangrey, who had still not married.

During the long and tiring journey to the palace, Rithisen took a nap. While he slept, a hermit appeared and read the secret message that Rithisen carried: "If Rithisen arrives during the day, he must be killed during the day. If he arrives at night, he must be killed at night." Seeing the treachery and danger, the hermit changed the message which Rithisen carried: "If Rithisen arrives during the day, Neang Kangrey must marry him during the day. If he arrives at night, Neang Kangrey must marry him at night." Rithisen arrived at the end of his journey and the changed message was read. A joyous wedding feast was organized to celebrate the union of the new prince and princess. But the new Prince Rithisen was unhappy, because his mind was constantly with his mother and aunts who would now be living without his care. Neang Kangrey tried to console him by showing him all the treasures in the palace, including the secret quarter where the eyes of his mother and aunts and magic medicines were kept.

That evening, as the wedding feast continued, everyone including Neang Kangrey celebrated until, exhausted, they fell deeply asleep. Prince Rithisen stole into the secret room, found the eyes in the special glass, and ran away into the night holding a bag containing the twelve pairs of eyes and magic medicine with which to cure his blind mother and her eleven sisters. In the morning, Neang Kangrey awoke to find Rithisen gone. She ordered a hunt to begin, and sent her army of soldiers out to find Rithisen. Broken-hearted and full of shame and desperation, Neang Kangrey brought her sad life to an end.

The mask of Giant. (Illustration by Yang Sam.)

"Loeung Preah Punlea" [Getting on the Pavilion]

Vocal (first verse)

Study Guide

Teaching/Learning Sequence   Level: Grade 4 through Adult

1. **Recall the instruments of the *mohori* ensemble,** in particular *khimm* (hammered dulcimer), *khloy* (flute), *roneat* (xylophone), *tror so* (two-stringed fiddles), *chhing* (small cymbals), and *thaun-rumanea* (drum pair). Note that there are no brass nor reed instruments of any sort in the *mohori* ensembles (See photo Chapter 9.)

2. **Tell the story of Neang Kangrey and Prince Rithisen.**
    * Play the recording of "Loeung Preah Punlea" to add to the story's flavor.

3. **For the music professional:** "Loeung Preah Punlea" is a typical Khmer piece whose melodic structure is based strictly on the pentatonic—and more precisely, the anhemitonic pentatonic scale. (The pentatonic scale has only five tones to its octave, and the anhemitonic pentatonic scale specifically refers to the five-tone scale devoid of semitones. Asian music, including Khmer, is prominently based on this kind of scale.)

➤While students conduct a four-beat pattern, play the melody for "Loeung Preah Punlea" on xylophone, or on piano.
    * How many measures of 4/4 comprise the melody? (16)
    * Does the melody contain slower and quicker sounds? (Yes) Is there syncopation in the melody? (Yes.)
    * Play the melody again as students conduct and check their responses.

➤Discuss the means by which the music expresses the feelings of Neang Kangrey on learning that her prince has taken leave of her. Note aspects of timbre, tempo, dynamics, mode and descending ornamental motif to longer, sustained pitches.

➤Listen to "Loeung Preah Punlea" in its six-part [AB AB AB] form that intermixes vocal with instrumental parts. Follow the melody for the vocal sections (although the aural and notated versions will vary somewhat.)
    * Consider the concept of overlapping in Khmer music: the gradual entrances of instruments toward the close of the vocal sections that link section A to section B; the overlapping of many melodic variants by the various instruments in section B.

A	Voice section with *chhing* and drums (16 measures)
	Gradual entrance of *khimm, tror so* and *roneat*
B	Instrumental section with *tror so, khimm, khloy, roneat, chhing,* drums. Simultaneous melodic variation
A	Voice section
B	Instrumental section
A	Voice section
B	Instrumental section

XI. The *Thaun-Rumanea*: Rhythmic Themes and Variations

Drums are important in Khmer music—they serve as leaders in the ensembles, and support the other pitched instruments; they set the tempo and keep the time for the ensemble. Yet, strangely enough, Khmer musicians do not tend to "major" in the drums during their training. Instead, they choose to study a melody instrument (like khloy, sralai or roneat), but become just familiar enough with certain drum patterns to be able to play them plainly and without much ornamentation. I play the various drums of Cambodia, including thaun-rumanea, but like other musicians, I have never studied them formally.

Students of the various Khmer drums first learn to say the rhythms they are about to learn to play, chanting onomatopoeic syllables in imitation of their teacher. The syllables sound like the various timbres produced by the drums, and are also indicative of the part of the drum head played, the fingers, palm, or head of the hand involved in the stroke, and the nature of the attack (sharp and quick versus muffled). These mnemonics are semantically meaningless syllables that act as aural cues to aid the memory, and they are extremely effective for the student who is working to master drum patterns on the various sizes of *sampho* and *thaun-rumanea*. The Khmer mnemonics include *choeung*, *chapp*, *ting*, *tup* and *theung*. Each has a pitch quality as it is articulated. The companion recording includes articulated mnemonics as well as basic and embellished drum patterns played on the *thaun-rumanea*. In the course of taking lessons a student will begin with the most basic pattern, repeated orally after hearing the teacher chant it. The teacher will then play as he chants, and expect that the student will again follow suit. This is not unlike percussion lessons in many other cultures. As the student masters the chanted and played examples, the teacher gradually moves on to more and more complex patterns, and then instruction in variation on the patterns.

The Khmer concept of rhythm in the practice of drumming is a cyclical one. That is, rhythm is prescribed and formed into patterns that repeat themselves in cycles. There are three rhythmic cycles: *muoy choan*, the first level rhythmic pattern of eight beats; *pi choan*, the second level rhythmic pattern of sixteen beats; and *bey choan*, the third level rhythmic pattern of thirty-two beats. A good drummer will develop variations upon the rhythmic pattern; the extent to which he can vary the pattern is the mark of an expert drummer.

The *thaun-rumanea* drum pair. (Photo by Sam-Ang Sam.)

105

Study Guide

Teaching/Learning Sequence   **Level: grade 4 - adult**

1. Explore further the idea of mnemonics, syllables that help one remember rhythms.
Many cultures use mnemonics as a tool to help musicians learn rhythms. Drum syllables or drum language is common throughout Africa; in the study of drums for the marching band, jazz or rock band using snare, toms or drum set; in Latin American timbale and conga patterns; even in rhythmic and melodic riffs played on all instruments in a jazz ensemble. Scat singing might have been a take-off on this technique.

* Create and share spoken rhythm patterns, then transfer the rhythms to table, body, or found percussion objects if instruments are not available.

2. Listen to the recording:

* Listen to the chanting of the rhythmic pattern. Recite the drum syllables slowly in rhythm. Use higher pitches for *ting, choeung* and *chapp* and a lower pitch for *theung.*

* Listen to the basic first level drum pattern of eight beats played four times. While reciting the drum syllables, play the pattern on lap, floor, or flat table-top:

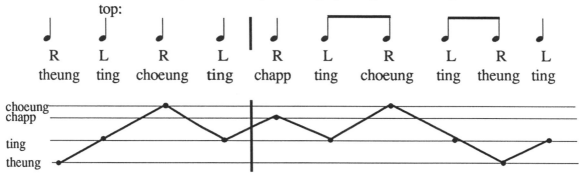

3. Find a high- and low-pitched sound on bongos, congas, table or body. Using hands rather than drum sticks or mallets, practice playing the basic drum patterns while reciting the drum syllables. Gradually, fade the syllables out so that just the drum's high and low pitches can be heard in the patterns.

4. For the music professional: Listen to the basic second level drum pattern of sixteen beats which is played twice, and also the variations on the sixteen-beat pattern which is also played twice. The basic second-level pattern is below:

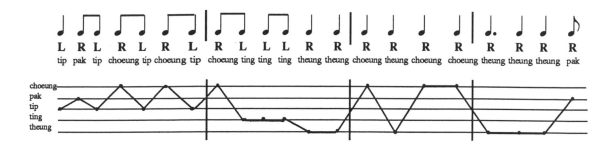

* Say the pattern in a call-and-response style.
* Say and play the pattern in a call-and-response style.
* Play the pattern without syllables, call-and-response style.
* Play the pattern as a group.
* Divide the class into two groups; some play the basic, some play the ornamented version of the eight-beat pattern and then in turn the sixteen-beat pattern can be treated the same way; individuals take turns playing variations while others continue the basic pattern.

XII. "Phleng Pradall": Boxing Music

I once attended a boxing match without hearing boxing music, and it was a dead event. The boxers need the music for movements in preparation for the fight, and also to guide their jumps, kicks, and jabs during the fight itself. Boxing in Cambodia is like dancing, and the music is key to the sport. Here in America I have not seen actual boxing matches, but I have presented a demonstration of boxing music with two boxers on the stage with the musicians, just to give the audience the idea. As far as I know, I am the only one who plays this boxing music in the United States.

Boxing is the most popular sport in Cambodia, with soccer rating a distant second place. No boxing match is complete without boxing music, traditionally played on the *sralai* (quadruple-reed shawm), the *sampho* (small barrel drum), and the *chhing*. Boxing is a men's event, and the boxers, musicians, and the audience in the stadium are mostly male. Boxers in their late teens through about the age of forty train in gym clubs and vie for slots in competitions and title bouts in the stadiums of Cambodia's larger cities.

Commonly, a boxing event has two parts to it. The first, which is called "English Style," features boxing as it is found in the United States, where the fighting is generally limited to use of the fists. There is no musical accompaniment for these matches. The second is "Free Style," and it is this which is always accompanied by boxing music. These events can go on for hours, match after match. If the event goes on for hours, the musicians play for hours, stopping only in between matches. Typically, the audience is grouped on three sides around the ring. The judges sit on the fourth side, perhaps on the main floor. The musicians sit at the back, behind the judges, or possibly on another level, and are usually not seen, depending on how the event is physically organized.

There is only one piece played for all boxing matches in Cambodia, and everyone who has ever attended a boxing match is familiar with it. The actual piece is titled "Klang Yaun," but most people don't know the correct title, and so refer to it simply as "Phleng Pradall" [Boxing Music]. The piece is in two sections: "Invocation to the Spirit" (of the boxer's *krou* [teacher]), and "The Fight." The invocation section is free-flowing and non-metered, and is played as the boxers perform a pantomime of movements in preparation for the fight; these movements may be as different from one another as acting out drawing a bow and arrow, or pretending to dress before a mirror. The musicians play until the boxers stop their movement, at which time the bell rings, and the fight proper begins. The music of the fight is quick, rhythmic and metric, punctuating and guiding the boxers' jumps, kicks and thrusts with their feet, elbows, head, knees and fists. As a boxing match reaches its peak, the music accelerates and the audience begins to clap wildly on the pulses of the *chhing*. Boxing and its music are distinctive traditions of the Khmer.

Study Guide
Teaching/Learning Sequence   Level: grade 2 - adult

1. Compare the description of Khmer boxing to boxing in other cultures. Other sports events elsewhere are accompanied by music that is considered typical. Explore examples of music for sports events in other parts of the world. What instruments and styles are associated with the music of various athletic endeavors? One unusual tradition is *capoeira,* a musical/martial art from Brazil, where the dancer/fighter is accompanied by the *berimbau,* a one-string/percussion instrument made of a long stick and gourd resonator that is plucked, struck, and pressed rhythmically against the body for special sound effects. Baseball games in America frequently include the spontaneous accompaniment of an organist. Many Chinese operas feature a stylized fight scene, choreographed to the music of drums and traditional instruments.

2. Listen to the recording:

* What instrument is playing the melody? [The introduction is performed on *sralai.*]

* What are some of the performance techniques of the *sralai*? [Listen particularly for sliding glissandos, raising and lowering of pitches.]

* Note that there are no rests or pauses in the playing of the melody. This is accomplished through circular breathing, described in detail in Chapter 3.

* Is it clear when "The Fight" section of the music begins? [You will hear the entrance of a regular pulse played by the *chhing.*]

3. For the Music Professional: In response to the music, listeners may wish to follow with their hands the rise and fall of the melody in the "Invocation to the Spirit" section, and to clap the pulse during "The Fight."

* Individuals may enjoy responding to the music with fighting movements.

Robaim tralok [coconut shell dance]. (Illustration by Yang Sam.)

XIII. *Roam Vung*: Popular Music/Popular Dance

Often when the Khmer gather for parties, roam vung music is played. I play electric bass in roam vung ensembles of guitars, keyboards, and drums. When not playing, I dance the roam vung, as do my wife and my daughters. It really has become the most frequently danced of all the dances of Cambodia, truly a national dance. Sometimes we rent a room in a hotel for an event. If the event is well-organized, there will be a table set with a vase of flowers in the middle of the dance area. We all dance in a large circle around the table and flowers. Sometimes there might not be a vase of flowers on a table, but we still dance in a large circle moving counterclockwise around a central point. I wrote the text and music for the roam vung song, "Anhcheunh Loeung Roam" [Please Get Up and Dance], featured on the companion tape.

Roam vung is a popular dance form in Cambodia and among Cambodians in the United States. Men, women and children perform *roam vung* at nearly every celebration, ceremony and social event. The origin of *roam vung* is unknown, but it is similar to a popular dance found in Thailand and Laos. In the more traditional settings, *roam vung* is accompanied by the *mohori* ensemble, with the goblet drum playing the rhythm. In urban communities, it is accompanied by the standard band of lead, rhythm, and bass guitars, keyboard, and drum set. The rhythm of *roam vung* is unique and can be immediately recognized by the Khmer people, but because of the instrumentation and beat it feels very mainstream American. During an evening of dancing, the Khmer usually include along with *roam vung* the *saravann* (a popular dance of Laotian origin), the Spanish bolero, and a series of Latin American cha-chas.

Roam vung is performed in a circle. People dance in male-female couples, with boys/men standing behind girls/women. Wives dance with husbands, boyfriends dance with girlfriends, and little boys may dance with their grandmothers. In the song on the companion recording, a woman sings of the music that has begun, and asks the men to join the dancers on the floor. The text tells of the beauty of the dance, the dancers, and of one particular man whom the woman likes. The singer also comments on the coordination of hand movements and footsteps with the song's rhythm.

Chann Chhaya Dance Pavilion. (Photo by Yang Sam, 1989.)

Malene Sam demonstrating the steps and gestures for *roam vung*. (Photos by Sam-Ang Sam.)

Study Guide
Teaching/Learning Sequence   Level: early childhood-adult

1. Listen to "Please Get Up and Dance." It is similar to mainstream American pop music in the choice of instruments used, and also in its rhythmic quality. It is different in language and text. Examine these and other similarities and differences between *roam vung* music and the music of your community and/or culture.

2. Learn the dance.

➤Move freely with the rhythm of the music, just absorbing the feel in your body.
  * Walk to the rhythm in any direction.

➤Practice the hand gestures of the dance. (See photos opposite.) Male dancers typically gesture larger than female dancers.
  * Walk freely in the rhythm adding the hand gestures.

➤Without the recording, practice the basic steps of the dance, standing in a circle facing to the right, men behind women. Walk forward as follows, beginning with weight on Right Foot (**R**).

Directions for *Roam Vung*

Key: R = right foot				L = left foot			
F = Forward (walk forward)				B = Back (Place foot behind foot of second beat.)			
	♩	♩	♩	𝄽	♩	♩	♩	𝄽
Begin with weight on Right Foot }	L	R	L	— /	R	L	R	—
	F	F	B	— /	F	F	B	—

(Chant the directions "Left, Right, Left, (Pause); Right Left, Right, (Pause)," and then, "Forward, Forward, Behind, (Pause); Forward, Forward, Behind, (Pause)," while stepping the pattern.)

➤Practice the steps with the recording.

➤Combine the foot, hands, and arm movements first without, then with the music. In pairs, dance *roam vung* as it is traditionally performed: in a large circle that moves counterclockwise around a vase of flowers set on a table.

XIV. The Legend of Tiger

Before the introduction of radio and television to Cambodia, we enjoyed telling stories for hours. In the evening after dinner, we children would sit together on a bamboo bed in front of the house to hear our parents' tales. We learned to tell stories in school, too. I remember stories of Mr. Rabbit's adventures with the snail, the crocodile and the tiger, and stories about the elephant and the ant, the bear and the fly, and the rooster and the toad. Mr. Rabbit is a very popular character in Khmer storytelling—a character who always comes to help when someone is in trouble. Today, unfortunately, storytelling has been largely replaced by television, radio, and films, but some are being written down so they will not be altogether forgotten.

Khmer literature is strongly tied to the daily lives of the Khmer people. Little children listen attentively to their grandparents' tales, which have been orally transmitted for many generations. When young Khmer leave home in early adolescence to study at Buddhist temples and monasteries called *vatt*, they learn to read and write the traditional literature. Prayers and didactic folktales and fables like the Buddhist *jataka* (the 550 life stories of the Buddha) are important to the young people of Cambodia. Outside the *vatt*, the Khmer are influenced by the stories presented in popular theater performances of the *lkhon basakk* (Chinese-influenced theater) and *lkhon yike* (folk theater).

The influence of Indian Brahmanism and Hinduism is also important to Khmer literature. The Reamker, the Khmer version of the great Indian legend of the Ramayana, is a prevalent theme in many of the performing arts, including court dances, mask plays and shadow puppet plays. It is also the basis for the inscription on the Angkor temples.

The Khmer are appreciative of their literature, as it plays a major part in guiding philosophy, attitude and behavior. Stories and poems are vehicles that influence the Khmer lifestyles—their day-to-day living patterns, their schooling, recreation and entertainment. The comic stories of Sophea Tunsay (Mr. Rabbit), Chao Chakk Smokk (The Dreamer), and "The Legend of Tiger" are examples of some of the important folktales drawn from an abundance of stories that children learn early on.

"The Legend of Tiger" is an important moral tale. It focuses on the necessity of individual cooperation for the general good, and makes clear the idea that a political body made up of members with different strengths who pledge mutual assistance is indeed a force to be reckoned with. Rulers who heed the contributions of their advisors, associates and family members rather than either forging ahead alone or distancing themselves from the issues of their country will find greater strength and lasting power. This is a didactic tale with the purpose of reminding the listener not to forget—not to turn his back on his country or community when things go so well he experiences increased wealth or extreme happiness. The Khmer say, "Don't get drowned in it," meaning don't drown in the happiness of the moment, or become drunk with power and forget to contribute anything to society. The king and his advisors and queen set out originally to learn magical powers for the benefit of their country, for if the king were to fall, the country would also fall. Their intention was to learn from the master and return to help the people and their country. But in the course of their magical transformation, they grew so enamored of the power of the tiger they drowned themselves in it, becoming Tiger forever, and in the end they contributed nothing.

Study Guide
Teaching/Learning Sequence   Level: early childhood - adult

1. **Listen to "The Legend of Tiger."** As it is told, try to imagine striking scenes of ancient Cambodia—its bejeweled and gold-laden courts of kings, queens, and royal personages, its dense green wetlands dotted with colorful flowers, trees, and exotic birds. As the characters appear, imagine how they might be dressed and what the sound of their voices might be as they speak. Why do you suppose this traditional tale is so highly regarded by the Khmer in Cambodia and abroad?

2. **Discuss some reasons why "The Legend of Tiger" has become an important moral tale.** Examine the magical transformation of the characters into the tiger. What are the tiger's virtues, and which character contributed them? Can obtaining power change people?
   * Try to find stories from other cultures that have a similar theme or storyline.

3. **Dramatize the story using the version that follows.** Choose group members to narrate and play the characters. Add to the Khmer flavor of the story by playing "Khvann Tung" (Lesson IX on the companion tape) as musical background to the story's unfolding.

Yang Sam

"Doeum Kamnoeut Ney Satt Khla" [The Legend of Tiger]

Once upon a time, there was a king who enjoyed the wealth in his great kingdom. A queen, four ministers, and an astrologer—who were the king's right hands—took responsibility for managing all the royal affairs in the country, including overseeing the mandarins and the royal concubines.

One day, the king became worried about his kingdom, because he did not have much military power and said to himself, "If there were enemies who came to invade my territories, the king would fall easily into their hands." One morning, the king came out of his royal chamber accompanied by the queen and called for a meeting with the ministers. That morning the king desired to learn the magical art with Master Disapamokkha in the kingdom of Takkasila. The queen, then the astrologer and the four ministers asked also to accompany the king. The next morning they all left for the kingdom of Takkasila.

On the seventh day they arrived at Takkasila, and began to search for Master Disapamokkha. Finally they found the master and asked to be taught the magical science, and the master accepted their request. The king, the queen, the astrologer, and the four ministers learned the art of transforming themselves into different forms without difficulty. They could become animals: Yaksa, the giant; Gandharva, a celestial musician; or Suparva, the mythical bird, as they pleased. When the instruction was completed the king asked the master for permission to return to their kingdom and then left Takkasila.

On the third day of their journey, as a result of their karma, they became lost and unable to cross the woods. Furthermore they were short of food supplies to make their ends meet and could eat only the fruit from trees. The king then asked the astrologer, the four ministers and also the queen, "What can we do? We cannot live like this and continue our journey."

"Here is my idea," answered the astrologer. According to the magical formulas that we learned together we can transform ourselves into a big wild beast. We will catch animals to feed ourselves, waiting until we get back to our kingdom, where we will take back our human forms."

The king, the queen, and the four ministers agreed and applauded the suggestion.

"Now," asked the king, "to form the body of a beast what part do each of you want to become?"

The four ministers asked to become the four legs.

The astrologer asked to become the tail, whereas the queen, she became the body.

The whole body of the beast was formed and the head was left for the king.

Deciding so, they recited the magical formulas and became a royal tiger. They pursued and caught deer and other animals to feed themselves. At a certain point of this happy stage they ceased to think about their kingdom and remained being tiger forever. This is why the tiger is the strongest of all animals. It can perceive things very effectively because its tail was the astrologer. The body is flexible and supple as it was formed from the queen. The majestic head, the most terrifying of all animals, was formed from the king who was the most powerful of all men. In the end the four strong and solid legs were the four ministers, who were considered to be the pillars of the throne.

Appendix: Transcriptions in the Key of Recorded Performance

"Doeur Roeu Keng"

Doeur roeu keng dang khluon oy trang trauv dam rang toan khluon neou

kmeng tuoh ang-kuy roeu muoy chhor leng yeung kmeng kmeng chhor oy trang khluon

"Leang Dai"

Boeu dai yeung pra lakk dey komm chapp cham ney roeu num a
mnea kam chatt pouch vea teup ban sokk

1
har pruoh mean me rok roeu sya kach khlaing kla pra ha yeung
san leang dai noeung toeuk muoy

2
ban. II. Dauch neh yeung trauv mni chan rouch komm khan doh noeung sa bou.

"Chapp Kaun Khleng"

Chapp kaun khleng pra leng kaun ak po pich nhek nhak kaun anh te muoy.

"Leak Kanseng"

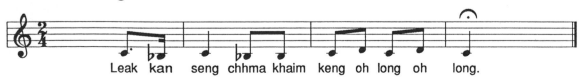

Leak kan seng chhma khaim keng oh long oh long.

117

"Chhoung"

Eu euy bang bah chhoung teou thlai euy chhoung teu leu chong

daung kra-momm chhor chraung thlai euy chaim chapp chhoung bang. Eu

euy o na keo keo pi a o na na na keo euy.

"Sarika Keo"

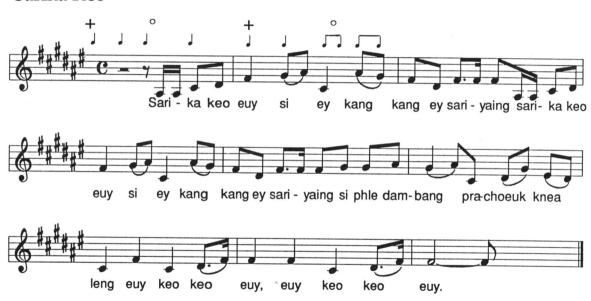

Sari - ka keo euy si ey kang kang ey sari - yaing sari- ka keo

euy si ey kang kang ey sari - yaing si phle dam-bang pra-choeuk knea

leng euy keo keo euy, euy keo keo euy.

"Thung Le"

"Khvann Tung"

Glossary

(Note: Although not indicated as such, the explanation of definition of the words gives the meaning in the Khmer context. For instance, court dance, folk dance, theater and king, all imply Khmer court dance, Khmer folk dance, Khmer theater, Khmer king, etc.)

A vorng euy	Phrase used to call a bird
Aha	Food
Ak	Bird; kind of vulture or eagle
Akk khan	To miss
Ang intri	Goddess
Angkor	Temple; capital city during the Angkor period (ninth-fifteenth centuries)
Angkor Vatt	Temple built during the thirteenth century by King Suryavarman II
Angkuy	To sit
Anh	I (first singular pronoun which could be impolite); mine
Anhcheunh Loeung Roam	Please Get Up and Dance; song title
Anlung	Hole
Apsara	Celestial nymph or dancer
Arakk	Worship of the spirit ceremony and ensemble
Arkun	Thank you
Ayai	Alternate singing
Ayuthaya	Capital city of Siam (fourteenth century)
Bah	To throw; to toss
Baing	To shade; to cover
Bakkha	Also called *baksa*; bird; song title
Baksa	Also called *bakkha*; bird; song title
Bamnak	Small town in Pursat province
Ban	To have; can

121

Bang	Title; big brother or sister; I (first singular pronoun more often used by a male person)
Basakk	Theatrical genre of Chinese influence and flavor
Bassac River	One of the four rivers (branches) which meets in Phnom Penh
Bat	Yes (men's term)
Battambang	Northwestern province of Cambodia
Be kich	To turn away hiding
Bey	Three
Bey choan	Three levels; level three
Bodhran	Irish flat frame drum similar to Khmer *rumanea*
Boeu	If
Bonn	Festival; ceremony; celebration
Bonn Cheat	National Day; national celebration
Bonn phka	Flower ceremony; fundraising ceremony
Bopha	Flower
Chah	Yes (women's term)
Chaim	To wait
Chakk kbach	To dance
Cham	Muslim; people of Champa
Chamney	Food
Champa	Cham kingdom prior to the seventeenth century; now part of Vietnam
Chan	Plate; bowl
Chang	Chordophone; Russian hammered dulcimer similar to Khmer *khimm*
Changrai	Misfortune; bad luck
Chao Chakk Smokk	The Box Braider (using strips of palm leaves) or The Dreamer; story title

Chapp	To catch; onomatopoeic drum syllable; sound produced by hitting a damped stroke in the middle of a goblet drum head
Chapp Kaun Khleng	Catch the Baby Eagle; game and song title
Chaul	To enter
Chaul Chhnaim	Khmer New Year which falls on April 13 in the Buddhist calendar; Khmer national holiday
Chea nich	Always
Cheat	Nation; national
Chenla	Ancient Khmer empire and historical period (sixth-ninth centuries) following the Funan
Chenn	Chinese
Chenn Choh Touk	Chinese Get on the Boat; song titlte
Chenn Se	Chinese Medical Doctor; song title
Chet	Hot month (April) when the Khmer celebrate their New Year
Chhepp	Closed *chhing* stroke
Chhing	Small cymbals; open *chhing* stroke
Chhloeuy chhlang	Dialogue; question-answer
Chhma	Cat
Chhnaim	Year
Chhor	To stand
Chhoung	Scarf ball used in game of the same name; game and song title
Chhouy Chhay	Proper name; song and dance title
Chik	To dig
Ching	Idiophone; Thai small cymbals similar to Khmer *chhing*
Choan	Level; layer; floor or story (building)
Choeung	Onomatopoeic drum syllable; sound produced by hitting the rim of a goblet drum head
Chong	End; top; summet

Chraung	Many; all; every; everywhere; all over
Chrieng	To sing
Chumreap lea	Goodbye
Chumreap suor	Hello
Cimbalom	Chordophone; Hungarian hammered dulcimer similar to Khmer *khimm*
Dai	Hand; arm
Daim	To plant; to grow
Damrang	To straight up
Dan tam thap luc	Chordophone; Vietnamese hammered dulcimer similar to Khmer *khimm*
Dang khluon	Body
Dauch	Like; as if
Dauchneh	So; thus; therefore
Daun	Old woman; grandmother
Daung	Coconut; coconut tree
Dek	To sleep (could be impolite)
Dett dall	To touch
Dey	Earth; soil; ground
Disapamokkha	Proper name; teacher of magical art in the kingdom of Takkasila
Doeum Kamnoeut Ney Satt Khla	Origin of Tiger; story title
Doeur	To walk
Doeur Roeu Keng	Walk or Sleep; song title
Doh	To wash; to clean
Duong haroeutey	Heart
Erh-hu	Chinese two-stringed fiddle similar to Khmer *tror so tauch*
Eu	Vocable

Euy	Vocable
Euy keo keo euy	Vocables
Ey	What
Ey sariyaing	Vocables
Founan	Ancient Khmer empire and historical period (first-sixth centuries)
Funan	(See Founan)
Funan-Chenla	Ancient Khmer empire and historical period (first-ninth centuries)
Gambang	Idiophone; Indonesian xylophone similar to Khmer *roneat*
Gandharva	Celestial musician
Hackbrett	Chordophone; Swiss hammered dulcimer similar to Khmer *khimm*
Hao	To call; to consider
Heng Samrin	Current President of The State of Cambodia
Jakay	Chordophone; Thai three-stringed zither similar to Khmer *krapeu*
Jataka	The 550 life stories of the Buddha
Jayavarman II	King of Cambodia (ninth century); founder of the Angkor dynasty
Jayavarman VII	King of Cambodia (thirteenth century); builder of the Bayon Temple (also known as Angkor Thomm); Khmer king who made Buddhism the state and national religion and who changed the practice of God-King to Buddha-King
Kach	Wild; cruel
Kambuja	Ancient and original name for Cambodia
Kambu Svayambhuva	The founder of Khmer dynasty, after whom Kambuja or Cambodia takes its name
Kamchatt	To get rid of; to eliminate; to terminate
Kampong Cham	Cambodian province

Kangrey	Proper name; female protagonist in the story of the same name; Prince Rithisen's wife
Kanjira	Membranophone; South Indian flat frame drum similar to Khmer *rumanea*
Kanseng	Scarf; handkerchief
Kapp	To axe; to cut with an axe or machete; to kill; to sacrifice
Kapp Krabey Phoeuk Sra	Buffalo Sacrifice; folk dance title
Kar	Wedding ceremony and ensemble
Karma	Action
Kaun	Baby; child
Keng	To sleep (polite term addressed by and to children)
Keng	Heel
Khaim	To bite
Khan	To miss
Khimm	Chordophone; hammered dulcimer
Khlaing kla	Strong; nasty
Khleng	Kite; bird of prey which feeds on baby chickens; kind of eagle
Khloy	Aerophone; duct or fipple flute
Khlui	Aerophone; Thai duct or fipple flute similar to Khmer *khloy*
Khluon	Body
Khmao dai	Pencil
Khmao dai muoy	One pencil
Khmao dai pi	Two pencils
Khmer	Cambodian; Cambodians
Khmer Changkeh Reav	Slim-Waisted Khmer; song title

Khmer Krang Phka	Khmer String Flowers; song title
Khmer Leu	Highlanders; the Pnorng (Phnong) minority group inhabiting the northeastern part of Cambodia in the provinces of Rattanakiri and Mondulkiri
Khmer Rouge	Communist Cambodians; genocidal movement and regime (led by Pol Pot) which was responsible for the killing of millions of Khmer lives
Khnang	Back (body)
Khnhomm	I (first singular pronoun)
Khong wong	Idiophone; Thai circular frame gongs similar to Khmer *korng vung*
Khvann Tung	Song title
Khyall Bakk Cheung Phnum	The wind Blows at the Foot of the Mountain; song title
Khyall Chumno Khe Praing	Breeze of the Dry Season; song title
Kim	Chordophone; Thai hammered dulcimer similar to Khmer *khimm*
Klahan	Brave; courageous
Klang Yaun	Suspended Drum; song title
Kmeng	Young
Kngok	Peacock; peahen
Kngok Posatt	Peacock of Pursat; folk dance title
Koat	He; she
Kokk	Egret
Komm	Negation; do not
Komm yum soka	Do not cry
Korng	Idiophone; gong
Korng tauch	Idiophone; high-pitched circular frame gongs
Korng thomm	Idiophone; low-pitched circular frame gongs
Korng vung	Idiophone; circular frame gongs
Kou	Pair
Krabey	Water buffalo

Krama	Scarf; piece of cloth of various sizes made of cotton or silk of different colors, usually with a striped pattern
Kramomm	Woman; the virgin; unmarried woman
Krapeu	Chordophone; three-stringed zither; crocodile
Krapeu Kantuy Veng	Long-Tailed Crocodile; song title
Krasa	Heron
Krou	Teacher
Kroy	At the back; back
Kruoch	Quail
Laim leav	Popular dance and rhythm
Laim thaun	Popular dance and rhythm
Lao Doeur Prey	Laotians Walk in the Forest; song title
Lbey	Famous
Leak	To hide
Leak Kanseng	Hiding the Scarf; game and song title
Leang	To wash; to clean
Leang Dai	Wash Hands; song title
Leng	To play
Leu	On top; at the top; on; above; over
Leuk	To raise; to rise; to lift
Lkhon	Theater; play
Lkhon basakk	Theatrical genre of Chinese influence and flavor
Lkhon kbach	Court dance
Lkhon khol	Masked play
Lkhon yike	Folk theater
Loah	To grow well
Loeung	To climb
Loeung Preah Punlea	Getting on the Pavilion; song title

Lok	Title; respected form of address for men
Lok Srey	Title; respected form of address for women
Lolork	Dove
Lon Nol	President of the Khmer Republic (1970-1975)
Lorp	To sneak
Mahabharata	Indian epic
Makk	Mother
Mean	To have
Mek	Branch
Mekong River	Main river in Cambodia whose four branches meet in Phnom Penh, giving the name to the present period of Khmer history the Chatomokk, which means "four faces"
Merok	Germs
Meul	To look at
Mi gyaun	Chordophone; Burmese three-stringed zither similar to Khmer *krapeu*
Minn	Negation; not
Mkott	Crown; headgear worn by dancer
Mni mnea	To hurry
Moan prey	Wild hen
Moat	Mouth; beak
Mohori	Name of a bird; music ensemble and repertoire; entertainment ensemble
Mon	Khmer race and ancestors
Mon-Khmer	Original race from which the present Khmer came
Msil minh	Yesterday
Muk	Face; front
Mun Pel Nhaim	Before Mealtime; song title
Muoy	One

Muoy choan	One level; level one
Neak	You (second singular and plural pronoun)
Neak phang	Other people; others
Neary neang	Lady; woman
Neou	To stay; to live; while
Ngeup	To raise up; to get up
Nhaim	To eat
Nhek nhak	To call
Nhonhimm	To smile
Nih	This
Nirvana	Enlightenment
Niyeay	To speak; to talk
Noam	To cause
Noeung	With; to
Norodom Sihanouk	King of Cambodia (1941); President of the Coalition Government; Head of the Supreme National Council (SNC)
Num	Cake; dessert
O na keo keo pi a	Vocables
O na na na keo euy	Vocables
Oeu	Yes (impolite term)
Oh	To drag; to pull; to draw
Oh long	To drag the leg
Oy	To give; to
Pattala	Idiophone; Burmese xylophone similar to Khmer *roneat*
Pel	Time
Pey	Aerophone; pipe
Pey pork	Aerophone; single free-reed pipe

Pey praboh	Aerophone; double-reed pipe
Phall	Produce
Phay phatt	To blow
Phchum Benn	Ancestral Day; Soul Day; Khmer religious ceremony
Phdaim	To tell
Phka	Flower
Phle dambang	Cactus fruit
Phleng	Music
Phleng kar	Wedding music
Phleng Manil	Manila music; origin of Khmer popular music
Phleng Pradall	Boxing Music; song title
Phleung	Fire
Phlomm	To blow; to play an aerophone
Phnom Penh	Present capital city of Cambodia
Phoeuk	To drink
Phtum	To sleep (royal term)
Pi	Aerophone; Thai quadruple-reed shawm similar to Khmer *sralai*
Pi	Two
Pi choan	Two levels; level two
Pidor	Fragrance
Pinn	Chordophone; angular harp
Pinn peat	Court ensemble and repertoire used to accompany court dance, masked play, shadow play, and religious ceremonies
Pisak	May (month)
Ploy	Aerophone; free-reed mouth organ
Pol Pot	Khmer Rouge leader (1975-1979)
Ponhea Yat	King of Cambodia (fifteenth century) who made Phnom Penh his capital

Popich	Kind of small bird
Por	Yes (monk's term)
Posatt	Pursat province; Khmer province in western Cambodia
Pothisatt	Bodhisatva; the enlightened one
Pouch	Race; species; crops
Prachoeuk knea	To nip at each other
Praha	To kill
Pralakk	Dirty
Praleng	To play with
Pramor	Tuning blob; a mixture of scraped lead, beeswax, and rosin
Pranhapp	To hurry
Preah	Buddha; title
Preah Chann Korup	Proper name; dance drama title
Preah Chinavung	Proper name; dance drama title
Preah peay	Wind
Proeuksa	Forest; wood; tree
Pruoh	Because
Puon	To hide
Pursat	Khmer province in the western part of Cambodia
Ramayana	Indian epic
Ranat	Idiophone; Thai xylophone similar to Khmer *roneat*
Reamker	Khmer version of the Ramayana
Riel	Cambodian currency (US$1=R1,000 in 1991)
Rithisen	Proper name; Prince; male protagonist in the story of Rithisen Neang Kangrey: Neang Kangrey's husband.
Roam	To dance
Roam kbach	Popular dance and rhythm
Roam vung	Dance in a circle; popular dance and rhythm

Roeu	Or
Roeusya	Cruel; nasty
Roneat	Idiophone; xylophone
Roneat dek	Idiophone; high-pitched metallophone
Roneat ek	Idiophone; high-pitched xylophone
Roneat thong	Idiophone; low-pitched metallophone
Roneat thung	Idiophone; low-pitched xylophone
Ruoch	Then
Rut	To run
Sa-at	Clean; neat; beautiful
Sabou	Soap
Sala	School
Saloma	Fight; combat; song title
Sambath	Proper name
Sampeah	To salute
Sampeah krou	To salute the teacher
Sampeah neak ta	To salute to the local guardian spirit
Sampho	Membranophone; small double-headed barrell drum
Samput	Skirt
Samput chang kbenn	Cotton or silk garment of different colors and designs wrapped around the waist with one end rolled, passed between the legs and fastened into a belt at the back
Samran	To sleep (polite term)
Santhamea	Proper name; giantess; Neang Kangrey's mother
Santir	Chordophone; Iranian hammered dulcimer similar to Khmer *khimm*
Santoor	Chordophone; Indian hammered dulcimer similar to Khmer *khimm*

Saravann	Popular dance and rhythm; name given after the Laotian province Saravane
Sarika keo	Small black bird with white and yellow markings on the sides of its head
Sarong	Cotton or silk single piece of material wrapped around the waist which falls down to the ankles; worn by both men and women
Saw duang	Chordophone; Thai high-pitched two-stringed fiddle similar to Khmer *tror chhe*
Sbek	Skin; hide; shadow play
Sbek tauch	Small skin; small hide; small-sized shadow play
Sbek thomm	Large skin; large hide; large-sized shadow play
Sdech Sok	Sad King; song title
Sek	Parrot
Sen	Very; too
Si	To eat (could be impolite)
Siem Reap	Ancient capital and important cultural center located in the northern part of Cambodia
Sinuon	Mixture of white and yellow colors; cool color; song title
Skor	Membranophone; drum
Skor arakk	Membranophone; goblet drum
Skor thomm	Membranophone; large double-headed barrell drum
Skor yol	Membranophone; suspended double-headed barrell drum
Slap	Wing
Sneng	Aerophone; horn
Soeung	To sleep (monk's term)
Sok	Proper name
Sokk sabbay te?	How are you?
Sokk sabbay te	I am fine

Sokk san	Safe; safety
Somm	To ask for
Sophea Tunsay	Mr. Rabbit; story title
Sra	Wine; alcoholic substance
Sralai	Aerophone; quadruple-reed shawm
Srey suor	Heavenly lady
Suparva	Mythical bird
Surin	Place name; lost province of Cambodia
Suryavarman II	King of Angkor who built the Angkor Vatt Temple
Taingyou	Kind of umbrella
Takkasila	Place name; kingdom
Te	Only
Teou	To go
Teou na?	Going where?; where are you going?
Teu	To get stuck
Teup	Then; just
Than	World; place
Thaun	Membranophone; goblet drum
Thaun-rumanea	Membranophone; drum pair (*thaun* and *rumanea*)
Theravada Buddhism	Branch of Buddhism (small vehicle) practiced by the Khmer; Cambodia's state and national religion
Thett	To reside; to stay; to live at
Theung	Onomatopoeic drum syllable; sound produced by hitting an open stroke in the middle of a goblet drum head
Thlai euy	My dear
Thngai	Day
Thngai nih	Today
Thung Le	Song title

Tien	Candle
Ting	Onomatopoeic drum syllable; sound produced by hitting an open stroke on the rim of a goblet drum head
Toan	While; on time
Toeuk	Water
Tonle Sap	Great Lake
Totea	Kind of bird similar to partridge
Totuol	To receive; to to pick up; to play (music)
Trakuon	Convolvulus; vine-like vegetable that grows in water
Trang	Straight
Trauv	Must; correct
Tror	Chordophone; stringed fiddle
Tror chhe	Chordophone; high-pitched two-stringed fiddle
Tror Khmer	Chordophone; three-stringed spike fiddle
Tror ou	Chordophone; low-pitched two-stringed fiddle
Tror so tauch	Chordophone; medium-high-pitched two-stringed fiddle
Tror so thomm	Chordophone; medium-low-pitched two-stringed fiddle
Tung	Pelican
Tunsay	Rabbit; hare
Tuoh	Whether; despite
Tup	Onomatopoeic drum syllable; sound produced by hitting a damped stroke on a flat frame drum
Thveu	To do; to make; to fabricate; to construct; to build
Vatt	Temple; pagoda; monastery where the Khmer worship
Vea	He; she; it; his; her; its
Vimean	Palace; pavilion; dwelling quarter
Yaksa	Giant; ogre

Yang chin	Chordophone; Chinese hammered dulcimer similar to Khmer *khimm*
Yangum	Chordophone; Korean hammered dulcimer similar to Khmer *khimm*
Yeamea	Heavenly world; heaven
Yeung	We; us

Selected Bibliography

(*Note*: For hard-to-find books, contact the Echols Collection of the Cornell University Library. Their collection of Southeast Asian materials is extensive.)

Anderson, William M. and Patricia Shehan Campbell, eds.
  Multicultural Perspectives in Music Education. Reston, VA: MENC, 1989.
Brandon, James.
  Brandon's Guide to Theatre in Asia. Honolulu: The University Press of Hawaii, 1976.

——————.
  Theatre in Southeast Asia. Cambridge: Harvard University Press, 1967.
Brunet, Jacques.
  "Nang Sbek: Danced Shadow Theatre of Cambodia," *The World of Music XI*, 4 (1969), 19-37.
Catlin, Amy.
  Apsara: The Feminine in Cambodian Art. Los Angeles: The Woman's Building, 1987.
Chandler, David.
  A HIstory of Cambodia. Boulder: Westview Press, 1983.

——————.
  The Land and Peoples of Cambodia. New York: J.B. Lippincott, 1972.
Chap, Pin.
  Jeux Populaires au Cambodge. Phnom Penh: Editions de l'Institut Bouddhique, 1964.
Coedes, George.
  Angkor. Singapore: Oxford University Press, 1963.
Cogniat, Raymond.
  Danse d'Indochine. Paris: Editions des Chroniques du Jour, 1932.
Cravath, Paul.
  "Earth in Flower: An Historical and Descriptive Study of the Classical Dance Drama of Cambodia." Ph.D. Dissertation, University of Hawaii, 1985.
Curtis, Grant.
  Cambodia: A Country Profile. Stockholm: Swedish International Development Authority, 1990.
Daniélou, Alain.
  Musique du Cambodge et du Laos. Pondichéry: Pulications de l'Institut Français d'Indologie, 1957.
Les Douze Jeunes Filles ou l'Histoire de Néang Kangrey. Phnom Penh: Editions de l'Institut Bouddhique, 1969.
Education. Phnom Penh: Ministry of Education, 1991.
Groslier, Georges. *Danseuses Cambodgiennes Anciennes et Modernes,* ed. Augustin Challamel. Paris: Maison Firmin-Didot, 1913.
Malm, William. *Music Cultures of the Pacific, the Near East, and Asia*. Englewood Cliffs: Prentice-Hall, 1967.
Marchal, Henri. "Note sur un Théâtre d'Ombres à Siem Réap," *Bulletin de la Société des Etudes Indochinoises XXXIII*, 3 (1958).

Marchal, Sappho.

    Costumes et Parures Khmères, ed. G. Vanoest. Paris: Librairie Nationale d'Art et d'Histoire, 1927.

————————.

    Danses Cambodgiennes. Saigon: Editions de la Revue Extrême-Orient, 1926.

Meyer, Charles.

    Royal Cambodian Ballet. Phnom Penh: Ministry of Information, 1963.

Musique Khmère. Phnom Penh: Imprimerie Sangkum Réastr Niyum, 1969.

Osman, Mohd Taib, ed.

    Traditional Drama and Music of Southeast Asia. Kuala Lumpur: Kementerian Pelajaran Malaysia, 1974.

Porée-Maspéro, Eveline.

    Cérémonies des Douze Mois. Paris: Centre de Documentation et de Recherche sur la Civilisation Khmère, 1985.

Sam, Chan Moly.

    Khmer Court Dance: A Comprehensive Study of Movements, Gestures, and Postures as Applied Techniques. Newington: Khmer Studies Institute, 1987.

Sam, Sam-Ang.

    "The Pin Peat Ensemble: Its History, Music, and Context." Ph.D. Dissertation, Wesleyan University, 1988.

Sam, Sam-Ang and Chan Moly Sam.

    Khmer Folk Dance. Newington: Khmer Studies Institute, 1987.

Sam, Yang.

    Khmer Buddhism and Politics from 1954 to 1984. Newington: Khmer Studies Institute, 1987.

Sam, Yang and Sam-Ang Sam.

    Children Songs. Phnom Penh: Bureau of Kindergarten of the Ministry of Education, 1972.

Sèm, Sara.

    "Lakhon Khol au Village de Vat Svay Andet, Son Role dans les Rites Agraires," *Annales de l'UBA*, 1 (1967), 157-200.

Southeast Asia II, 2nd ed. New York: Greystone Press, 1969.

Steinberg, David.

    Cambodia: Its People, Its Society, Its Culture. New Haven: Human Relations Area Files, 1959.

Thierry, Solange.

    Les Danses Sacrées. Paris: Sources Orientales, 1963.

Thiounn (Samdach Chaufea).

    Danses Cambodgiennes. Phnom Penh: Editions de l'Institut Bouddhique, 1956.

Vincent, Frank.

    The Land of the White Elephant. New York: Harper and Brothers, 1874.

The World Fact Book 1988. Washington, DC: CIA, 1988.

Zarina, Xenia.

    Classic Dances of the Orient. New York: Crown Publishers, 1967.

Selected Discography

(*Note*: Many of these are available in university music libraries, through the University of Washington Southeast Asian Studies Department, Cornell University Library, or the Khmer Studies Institute. Several are current and easy to obtain.)

Anthologie de la Musique du Cambodge. Ducretet-Thomson DUC 20-21-22.

Cambodge. Galloway GB 600520.

Cambodge: Musique Instrumentale. Columbia Broadcasting System CBS 65522.

Cambodge: Musique Samrê des Cardamomes. La Boite a Musique LD 112.

Cambodia. Barenreiter BM 30 L2002.

Cambodia. Musical Atlas EMI C-064-17841.

Gongs: Asie du Sud-Est. Columbia Broadcasting System CBS 65964.

Mohori: Khmer Entertainment Music. Khmer Studies Institute M91-SS-NR002.

Music of Cambodia. World Music Institute WMI-007.

Musique du Cambodge des Forêts. Anthologie de la Musique des Peuples AMP 2902.

Musique et Danse au Cambodge. Harmonia Mundi 50-51.

Patriotic and Traditional Khmer Songs. Cambodian Business Corp. Int'l PTKS-SS-NT001.

Royal Music of Cambodia. Philips 6586 002.

Traditional Music of Cambodia. Center for the Study of Khmer Culture TMC-SS-NR001.

Selected Filmography

(*Note*: The Khmer Studies Institute has an extensive archive of films, books, photographs and articles. Address: Khmer Studies Institute, Inc. PO Box 11-497, Newington CT 06111-0497.)

Classical and Folk Dances. Ministry of Information and Culture, 1986. (Avail. UWash. Dept. of Southeast Asian Studies.)

Classical Khmer Ballet of Cambodia. Brooklyn Academy of Music, 1971.**

Dance Troupe of the University of Fine Arts from the State of Cambodia. The Los Angeles Festival, 1990. (Avail. UCLA World Arts and Cultures Program.)

The Goddess Dancer of Cambodia. Camera Three (CBS), 1973.

Princesses d'Angkor. Cinémathèque de la Coopération, 1938. **

The Royal Ballet of Cambodia. Asia Dance Project (John D. Rockefeller, III Fund).**

** Available through the Film Archives of the Dance Collection at Lincoln Center Library of the Performing Arts, New York City.

Index

Accents: language, 30; musical, 40
Agriculture, 23
Angkor period, 24, 39
Angkor Vatt, 28,35,39,48,
Apsara, 35,39,

Bakkha (Baksa), 80-83, *82*
banjo, 89
Birds, 21, 76, 80
Bodhran, 45
Bonzes [monks], 29,31,32,
Boxing Music, 50, 108-110
Buddhism, 83; Theravada, 27, 29, 35

Cambodia,
　　Climate, 21, 87
　　Economy, 23
　　Education, 34
　　Ethnic make-up, 29
　　Exodus from, 25
　　Geography, 21
　　History, 23
　　Immigrants and Refugees from, 25, 52, 53
　　Language, 30
　　Maps, 20

Chapp Kaun Khleng, 67-71,*68, 117*
Children's songs, 63-67
Chhing, 39, 105
Chhoung, 70, 72, 75, *118*
Chordophones, 46-47
Circular breathing,41-42
Classical dance, see: court dance
Clothing, 31, 72
Comparisons of Khmer music with other styles, 39
Costumes, 35,48,

Court dance, see Dance, court
Dance,
　　Court, 35, 39, 48, 49, 53, 80, 81, 83
　　Folk, 49, 50, 53, 110
　　Popular, 53
　　Roam vung,
Doeur Roeu Keng, 63, *64, 117*
Drums, 39, 45, 46, (see: instruments: membranaphones)

Education, 34

Family life, 30, 31
Festivals, 31-33
Fiddles, 46, *47,* 87
Folk dance, see Dance, Folk
Foods, 23
France, 23, 24, 34
Funan 24, 25

Game songs, 67-70, 71-75,
Giant, *101, 102*

Indonesia, 87, 88, 89
Instruments, 37-56, 84, 86, 87-90
　　Aerophones: *khloy, pey pork, sralai,*41-42
　　Chordophones, *khimm, krapeu, tror chhe, tror Khmer, tror ou, tror so tauch, tror so thomm,* 46-47
　　Idiophones, 39, 42-45
　　korng tauch, korng thomm, korng vung, roneat, roneat ek, roneat thung,
　　Materials found in, 87, 89
　　Membranophones,45-46
　　sampho, skor arakk, thaun-rumanea

Jacob's Pillow, 53
Jayavarman II, 24
Jayavarman VII, 24,

Khloy, 41, 61, 84
Khmer, usage of, 15
Khmer, language, 30
Khmer Changkeh Reav, 92, 92-95
Khvann Tung, 98-100, *119*
Korng vung, 42
krama, 31, 72

Laos, 20, 21, 24, 31, 87
Leak Kanseng, 71, 117
Leang Dai, 63, 117
Legends, 114

Masked play, 90
Mekong, 22, 23,
Meter, musical, 40,
Mkott, 49
Mnemonics, 105, 106,
Mohori, 45, 96-100, 101, 104,
Monsoons, 21
Mun Pel Nhaim, 63
Musical: characteristics, 39; forms, 39-56;
        history, 39
        genres, 48; rock and pop, 54
Musical notation, 55,
Musicians: Cambodian, in the U.S., 52, 53

Orff, Carl, instruments, 61, 82, 83, 94
Ornamentation,40, 55, 83

Pey pork, 41
Phleng kar, 51
Pinn peat ensemble, 39, 91
Pol Pot, 24, 52
Popular music, 111
Pramor, 45
Prince Rithisen, 101-104
Pronunciation Guide, 17

Reamker,36, 48
Religion, 27, 29, 35
Roam vung, 54, 111-113
Roneat, 42, 84, 87, 91
Sachs-Hornbostel Classification System, 89
Sarika Keo, 76-79, *77*
Sampho, 39, 44, 45,
Scales,39
        pentatonic, 39
        heptatonic, 39
Scarves, symbolic role of, 74
Shadow play, 36, 56, 90
Shadow puppets, 36, 56
Shawm, (see *sralai*) 84,108, 109, 87
Songs: children's, 63-79

Sralai, 87, 88, 89, 90108, 109
Stories: in music, 90;
        Legend of Tiger, The, 114;
        Story of Neang Kangrey, The, 101

Teaching music, the process of, 42, 48, 52,
55, 59, 61, 91
Thai, Thailand, 20, 21, 31, 45, 87
Thaun-rumanea drum pair, 45,105
Thung Le, 86
Tradition and change, 52
Transcription,
        Guide to language, 17
        Notes on musical, 15-16
Trees, typical, 21

Vatt, 35,39
Vietnam, 29, 87

Wedding music, see: *phleng kar*
Weddings, 51, 53

Xylophones, 45, 84, 87, 88, 91-95,96